HAYNES **MAX** POWER **Citroën**

saxo

The definitive guide to **modifying**

by **Lou Brown & Bob Jex**

HAYNES MAX POWER Citroën

saxo

The definitive guide to modifying
by Lou Brown & Bob Jex

Haynes Publishing

ISBN 1 85960 908 2

Printed by **J H Haynes & Co Ltd,**
Sparkford, Yeovil, Somerset BA22 7JJ, England.

Tel: 01963 442030 Fax: 01963 440001
Int. tel: +44 1963 442030 Fax: +44 1963 440001
E-mail: sales@haynes-manuals.co.uk
Web site: www.haynes.co.uk

Haynes North America, Inc
861 Lawrence Drive, Newbury Park, California 91320, USA

Editions Haynes S.A.
Tour Aurore IBC - La Défense 2, 18 Place des Reflets,
92975 PARIS LA DEFENSE Cedex, France

Haynes Publishing Nordiska AB
Box 1504, 751 45 UPPSALA, Sweden

It wasn't my idea guv'nor!

1 Advice on safety procedures and precautions is contained throughout this manual, and more specifically on page 194. You are strongly recommended to note these comments, and to pay close attention to any instructions that may be given by the parts supplier.

2 J H Haynes recommends that vehicle modification should only be undertaken by individuals with experience of vehicle mechanics; if you are unsure as to how to go about the modification, advice should be sought from a competent and experienced individual. Any queries regarding modification should be addressed to the product manufacturer concerned, and not to J H Haynes, nor the vehicle manufacturer.

3 The instructions in this manual are followed at the risk of the reader who remains fully and solely responsible for the safety, roadworthiness and legality of his/her vehicle. Thus J H Haynes are giving only non-specific advice in this respect.

4 When modifying a car it is important to bear in mind the legal responsibilities placed on the owners, driver and modifiers of cars, including, but not limited to, the Road Traffic Act 1988. IN PARTICULAR, IT IS AN OFFENCE TO DRIVE ON A PUBLIC ROAD A VEHICLE WHICH IS NOT INSURED OR WHICH DOES NOT COMPLY WITH THE CONSTRUCTION AND USE REGULATIONS, OR WHICH IS DANGEROUS AND MAY CAUSE INJURY TO ANY PERSON, OR WHICH DOES NOT HOLD A CURRENT MOT CERTIFICATE OR DISPLAY A VALID TAX DISC.

5 The safety of any alteration and its compliance with construction and use regulations should be checked before a modified vehicle is sold as it may be an offence to sell a vehicle which is not roadworthy.

6 Any advice provided is correct to the best of our knowledge at the time of publication, but the reader should pay particular attention to any changes of specification to the vehicles, or parts, which can occur without notice.

7 Alterations to vehicles should be disclosed to insurers and licensing authorities, and legal advice taken from the police, vehicle testing centres, or appropriate regulatory bodies.

8 The vehicle has been chosen for this project as it is one of those most widely modified by its owners, and readers should not assume that the vehicle manufacturers have given their approval to the modifications.

9 Neither J H Haynes nor the manufacturers give any warranty as to the safety of a vehicle after alterations, such as those contained in this book, have been made. J H Haynes will not accept liability for any economic loss, damage to property or death and personal injury arising from use of this manual other than in respect of injury or death resulting directly from J H Haynes' negligence.

Contents

Haynes
Max Power

Buyer's guide

Insurance

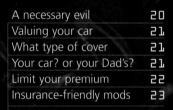

08 Suspension

09 Brakes

10 Interiors

Security

04

Body styling

05

Lights & bulbs

06

Wheels & tyres

07

11

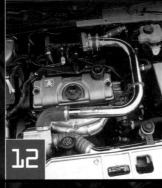

12

13

14

ICE

Engines

Exhausts

Reference

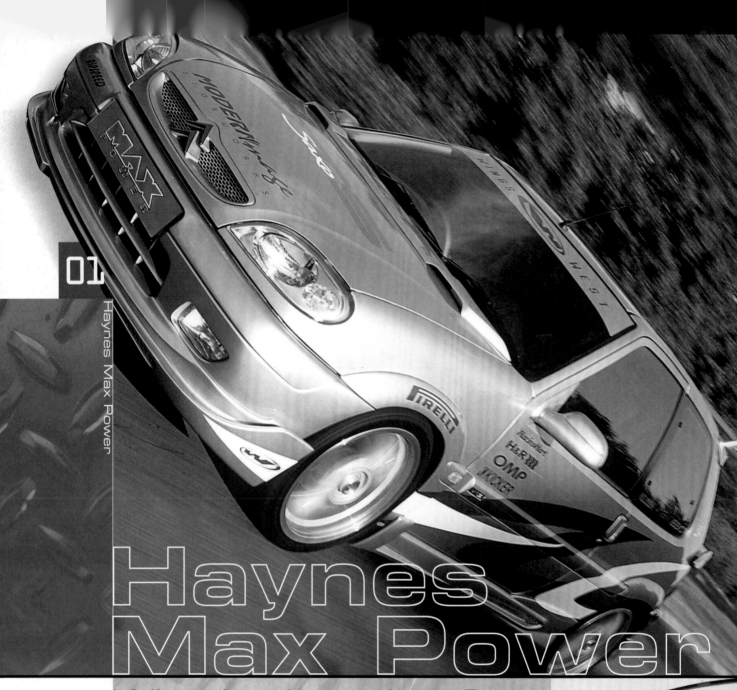

Haynes
Max Power

What's that then?

Haynes Publishing have, for the last forty years, been helping people keep their cars on the roads in countries all over the world by publishing maintenance manuals. Chances are you've either got one of them yourself or you know somebody who has.

"Lights & bulbs" includes fitting high-power blue headlight bulbs, coloured rear light clusters, etc.

Before

After

Remember what it feels like on your birthday, or at Christmas, when you're faced by a pile of pressies? So do we, that gnawing feeling in your gut, what's in them? What did I get? Take that feeling and multiply it by twelve, that's how we felt when we started this project. When we decided that it was time to try something new, we couldn't wait. Because the same theories apply to modifying your car as servicing it, we reckoned we'd better get on and do it ourselves. We don't pay other people to do it for us, and we get the same dodgy instructions with kit as everybody else.

So if you've ever wondered how to fit a universal door mirror properly, smooth a tailgate or just bolt a seat in, this book is for you.

We've picked up a skip full of tips along the way, and they're all here for you to use. We haven't tried to set any trends, but we've covered every possible process we think you'll need. So where we've tinted a front door window, the same rules apply to a rear one, job done.

If you look in the magazines and want some of that, join us, 'cos so do we, and we'll show you how to get it.

Keeping it real

Modifying a car is not without its problems in the 'real world', as opposed to the seemingly fantasy world of the glossy mags. For instance, it's pretty silly to spend hours fitting illegal window tints or smoked lights if you get pulled the first time you're out afterwards. Of course, you can get pulled for all sorts of reasons (and just driving a modified car is reason enough sometimes), but keeping the car actually legal is one of the 'hidden' challenges with modifying. Throughout the book, our tips should give all the help you need to at least appear to be on the right side of the law. The annual MOT test is another favourite time for your mods to get panned, and again, we aim to give you all the help necessary to ensure at least that what you've changed doesn't lead to a fail.

Security is another major issue with a tweaked motor, and the perils of insurance cannot be taken lightly, either. We aim to give down-to-earth advice to help you keep the car in the first place, and to help you in not upsetting your insurers too much if the worst happens.

A word about fashion

In producing this book, we're aware that fashions change. What we show being fitted to our car might well be hideously out of date in 6 months time, or might not be your thing in the first place. Also, some of the stuff we've acquired from our various suppliers may no longer be available by the time you read this. We hope that, despite this, our approach of showing you step-by-step how to fit the various parts will mean that, even if the parts change slightly, the procedures we show for fitting will still be valid.

Our main project car was a "Phase II" 1.6 litre VTR, 2000 W reg, with some additional work being carried out on other Saxos.

"Wheels & tyres" takes a detailed look at all the options.

"Body styling" shows you how to fit universal mirrors to full body kits.

"Interiors" includes seats, painting trim, gear knobs and loads more.

Citroën AX GT

The affordable hot hatch

Before the arrival of the AX GT in 1988, Citroën's record as a maker of hot hatchbacks was not the greatest. Anyone remember the oh-so-ugly Visa GTi? Thought not. Or how about the almost-as-attractive BX GTi 16V, with boxy bodykit?

With the AX GT, Citroën cleverly spotted a gap in the market that was about to be left by the long-time budget hot-hatch kings Ford, and the car was a great success. Although "only" a carb 1.4 litre, the AX's light weight meant it could see off more powerful opposition, and its lack of "cubes" kept the insurance crew happy. For young drivers, affordable fun, so long the key strength of the XR2 and XR3i (both soon to move upmarket and out of reach), was back!

As the years went on, the AX GT became the GTi, with fuel injection giving an even better power-to-weight ratio (at a slight extra cost on the insurance). Citroën seemingly began to lose interest in the AX though, and the "hot" models also went into a decline - they actually disappeared completely, two years before the demise of the whole AX range in 1996.

Citroën Saxo

The affordable hot hatch 2 - the sequel

Who says sequels never live up to the original? With the arrival of the new Saxo range in May 1996 came "teaser" press-release photos of the sexy new hot models, even though the cars never actually reached British roads until January 1997. An instant hit with press and public alike, the new VTR and VTS were hailed as the kings of the "new breed" of hot hatches. The hot hatch market had been in decline during the early Nineties, mainly because of stupid insurance premiums, but not any more!

Again using a clever marketing strategy, Citroën produced two near-identical-looking models with two distinct agendas. The VTS was the all-out go-for-it model, with a 120 bhp 16-valve 1.6 engine (and a Group 14 insurance rating to go with it) - clearly an "aspirational" model for new young drivers. The real success story sales-wise has been the "warm-hatch", "insurance-friendly" Saxo, the VTR, which has often been lauded as the best-selling hot hatch in Britain - and no cruise-goers in the last few years would argue

with that, they're everywhere! The VTR is almost identical to the VTS in every way, except in what's under the bonnet. Instead of the fire-breathing 120 bhp unit, we have an 8-valve 90 bhp 1.6 motor - still hardly a cause for embarrassment at the lights, and in Group 7, the insurance is seven groups lower than the VTS! The "lesser" model is also a useful two grand cheaper, and Citroën dealers are always offering attractive finance or free-insurance packages to bring even brand-new cars within reach of young drivers.

The Saxo was spawned from the newly-updated Peugeot 106 range (which itself has a pocket-rocket GTi model), but the approach Citroën have taken to marketing the hot models has put the 106 GTi in the shade on the sales front. Peugeot haven't really exploited the "affordable" angle as well as Citroën, and the pricey 106 GTi is really only a rival for the Saxo VTS.

With the success of the VTR and VTS, Citroën have acknowledged the existence of the young car modifier, and almost uniquely among car makers, actually support and encourage the modifying scene, with official Citroën Motorsport parts available - that you'd actually want to fit!

Never content to leave a good thing alone, Citroën facelifted the Saxo in 1999. The "Phase II" models met with some resistance among the modifying fraternity at first - not everyone liked the new front-end treatment - but the car's essential qualities have seen to it that sales haven't really suffered.

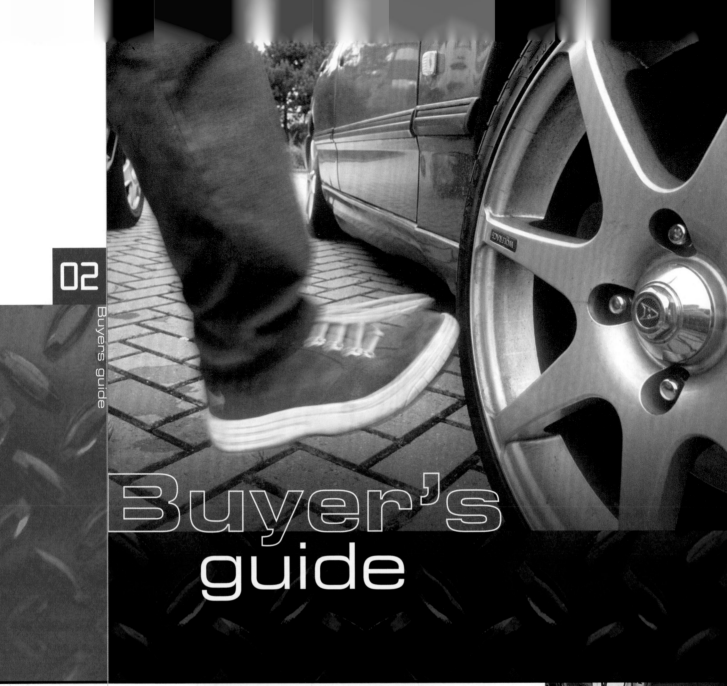

Buyer's guide

Where to start?

The first step is to decide which model of Saxo to go for. How big's your wad?

A good starting point is to phone around for a few insurance quotes for the different models and engine sizes available. As we all know, no insurance premium is ever going to be pleasant, but some are a whole lot more pleasant (or should that be "bearable") than others. There's no point owning a top motor only to find no one will insure you to drive it. Decide how much of your budget you're prepared to spend on insurance, and this will give you a rough idea of what's left over. When it comes to insurance companies, always expect the worst and you'll probably never be disappointed. A small point, but always remember that insurance is for a year only. What you have to stump up this year, you'll have to find again in twelve months' time, and as smart as your car may be, is it really worth going without food/drink, etc. for the next twelve months?

The range

Citroën originally introduced the Saxo in May `96 to replace the old AX model. The Saxo shares a lot of mechanical components with its predecessor, and was produced in both 3- and 5-door versions. The 5-door models - we'll immediately forget.

The model range consists of the bottom-of-the-range X and LX models, the mid-range SX model to the top of the range VSX or Exclusive. Add to these the sports VTR and VTS models, and there really is a Saxo to suit everybody.

The X and LX models come complete with doors and windows as standard equipment and little else, the SX has electric front windows, a sunroof and rev counter, and the VSX and Exclusive add to that extras such as electric mirrors, front foglights, remote central locking and power steering on most models. Standard equipment on the VTR and VTS models includes all the usual items (alloys, front foglights, sports seats, rear disc brakes, etc). The VTS also comes with ABS (Anti-lock Braking System) and electric mirrors as standard. To confuse things, Citroën also brought out a load of "Special Edition" models. These are tasteful little models with catchy names such as Scandal, Spree, Mischief, Desire and Expose, with supposedly-tasteful graphics and interior trim. Spec varies from model to model, but ultimately they're not usually worth more than a pop-up sunroof.

In late `99, the "Phase II" Saxo was introduced. Mechanically unchanged, but with a re-shaped front end featuring a larger, more rounded bonnet with an integral grille and redesigned headlights for a more up-to-date look. Worth the extra cash if you can afford it (but many modifiers prefer the simpler style of the "Phase I", so don't feel too bad if you can't).

Engine choices consist of 1.0, 1.1, 1.4 and 1.6 litre petrol engines, and (ahem!) a 1.5 litre diesel engine.

Base models

1.0 and 1.1 litre - the 1.0 litre (954 cc) and 1.1 litre (1124 cc) models are obviously the most insurance-friendly models in the range (Group 3 to 5 - depending on spec). That being said, neither is going to set the world alight in performance terms. The 1.0 litre engine pushes out 50 bhp and will get you from 0-60 in half an hour (around 18 secs, top speed is around 85 mph). The 1.1 litre engine improves on that slightly, kicking out 60 bhp which will get you from 0-60 slightly quicker in 14.5 secs and see a top speed of around 102 mph.

Obviously not a consideration for the power-crazed amongst you, but that doesn't mean they can't be made to look the part!

1.4 litre - altogether a much better option. The 1.4 litre (1360 cc) engine still remains quite insurance-friendly (Group 4 to 6 - depending on spec) but pushes out a more healthy 75 bhp. This results in a more respectable 0-60 time of 11.9 secs and a top speed of 109 mph. A popular choice in the limited-edition models is the West Coast, which came with the 1.4 engine and a wild Zest Yellow paint job - if you can find one, it's a great starting point for a cool set of wheels. Another model to keep an eye out for is the Furio introduced in early 2000. The Furio is basically a VTR look-a-like with a 1.4 litre engine - smart but insurance-friendly.

1.6 litre - not really an option (VTR/VTS models excepted - we'll come to those later!) since it's only available with an automatic gearbox. Shame really, 'cause with another 15 bhp (90 bhp) over the 1.4 litre engine, whilst remaining quite insurance-friendly, it would otherwise be the engine of choice for a few.

1.5 litre diesel - if you want a car that sounds like a taxi/tractor/lorry, this is the one for you. Very insurance-friendly, very economical, very slow, very noisy and exceptionally dull. Enough said!

Sports models

Now we're talking! The VTR and VTS are what every self-respecting lad aspires to, funds permitting. Cosmetically very similar, both are top motors, both fitted with a 1.6 litre engine, but there the underbonnet similarity ends. The VTR has the SOHC (Single OverHead Camshaft) 8-valve engine which kicks out 90 bhp, while the VTS has the DOHC (Double OverHead Camshaft) 16-valve engine producing a very healthy 120 bhp.

For the power-hungry amongst you, there can be only one choice; reaching 0-60 in 7.2 seconds and topping 127 mph, the VTS is the only model likely to be on your shopping list. But the VTR's no slug - in the real world, 0-60 in 9.3 seconds and a top speed of 116 mph is more than reasonable. In addition to this, both engines can both be easily tweaked to produce a fair bit more power with a few sensible mods.

What makes the VTR by far the more popular choice over the VTS (the VTR is "Britain's favourite hot hatch", apparently) is that it is much cheaper to insure. We're not talking a few quid less either - the VTR's in insurance group 7, while the VTS is in group 14. Seven insurance groups translates into a serious amount of extra cash every year - and for what? So before you set your heart on that VTS, you'd be well advised to get a few quotes.

Buying new?
Step this way, Sir

Depending on your budget, this may not be an option. However, before resigning yourself to second-hand, read on. Nowadays, your local dealership is not the only way to purchase a new vehicle, as much as they'd like you to think it is. For convenience and service, maybe a franchised dealership is the best option, but for value-for-money, there are other options.

Franchised dealers - the safe option

The most obvious way to purchase a new vehicle is to take a trip to your local franchised dealership, part with the necessary cash and drive out in a spanking new car. That way, you're guaranteed the best aftersales service/warranty back-up available. In theory. But as we all know, quality costs, and that service is supplied at your expense. It may well be possible to haggle a few hundred quid off the screen price of a new Saxo at your local dealership, but expecting to knock him down a few grand is, to say the least, being a bit optimistic. But hey, anything's worth a go!

To offset the cost aspect of buying from a dealership, the makers often offer incentive schemes, especially in the quieter sales periods. The most attractive incentive schemes are those offering free insurance or servicing for a year or two, or 0% finance on the car. These options will save you useful sums of cash, which you can then put to better use! Check the small print of all incentive schemes, but if a year's free insurance saves you a grand, you've essentially knocked a grand off the cost of the car. Suddenly, that year-old second-hand car ain't such a bargain after all.

One thing to check with the dealership is how any modifications you intend to make will affect the warranty (or insurance cover) given with the car. Engine mods will certainly invalidate the warranty, but will other changes also be used as an excuse to avoid settling any claims which arise?

Importing? Risks are not without reward

The first option is to import a UK-spec vehicle from Europe. On the continent, it's possible to pick up the same-spec vehicle (right-hand drive and with the same options) as your local dealer, but for tons less cash. Savings can be between 10 and 30%, more on some cars. That's four-figure sums, on a top Saxo. Interested? Thought so.

The best way to import is through one of the many specialists. The importing lark is now big business, from large set-ups (Virgin Cars, JamJar), to the smaller operations run by a couple of blokes operating from a lock-up in Brixton. Check out all the small print before placing your order and parting with your deposit. As well as the all-important price, check out the vehicle warranty, the expected delivery date/waiting time (is this guaranteed, or just an estimate?), deposit required, any other booking fees/administration costs, and what kind of aftersales service they offer. You might find that top deal may not be the wisest choice after all.

There are risks with an import, but with a little bit of research, these risks can be minimised. Obviously the guy operating from a lock-up will be cheaper than the big boys, but will he still be there in six months' time, or sat on a beach in the Caribbean on your deposit? Always do all transactions on a credit card - that way, you should have some sort of comeback, should the worst happen. If the geezer on the phone quotes you two grand cheaper than anyone else, then asks for the deposit in used bank notes to a PO Box of his choice, we suggest you re-consider.

The car supermarket. D'you want beans with that?

Car supermarkets are huge operations which import UK-spec vehicles in great numbers, and knock them out for bargain prices. Such a simple concept, it makes you wonder why it didn't happen years ago.

The drawback is that if you have very specific requirements (like a specific model in a certain colour with a specific options pack), the car supermarket is probably not the place to shop. These places operate on a first-come, first-served basis, and will not order-in specific cars. What you see is what you get, and the price is exactly what is says on the screen. Don't bother haggling - these places operate on selling huge numbers of vehicle at very low profit margins. They don't inflate the screen price just so you can feel good when you get a few hundred quid off. When was the last time you haggled over the price of a tin of beans at Tesco?

The car supermarket is a relatively recent phenomenon, and as such, there aren't many in the country. Unless you live around the London area or in the Midlands, you're in for a long trip. Will you also get the full factory warranty, so you can visit your local dealer for warranty work, or will that too mean a long trip every time?

If you're prepared to be a bit flexible as to model/colour options and are prepared to buy on the spot, a day out at the supermarket could be a very rewarding experience. Just don't expect any buy-one-get-one-free offers!

Used car - more left over for essential extras

Not enough cash for a new car, or just want more of your wad to spend on bolt-on goodies? A used motor is the way to go. Even if money is no object, the second-hand route is a better choice to avoid the restrictions of the maker's warranty or being tied into having it serviced by an ever-so obliging, but pricey, main dealer.

Buying a used Saxo isn't as risky as some other vehicles. The whole range consists of tried-and-tested engineering used in many other Citroën and Peugeot vehicles over the years. Basically, the Saxo is a development of the old Citroën AX and Peugeot 106. As such, there's little to be wary of in the way of mechanical gremlins, so long as it's been serviced correctly, and reasonably well-cared-for. Since the Saxo only dates back to May 1996, there's no need to worry about rust. Come the mid-1990s, all the makers had pretty well sorted out their anti-corrosion treatments, so rot shouldn't be a problem for a few years yet - any rot you do see will likely point to badly-repaired accident damage, so walk away.

Used car dealers.
Dodgy blokes in sheepskin jackets?

The safest way to make your prospective purchase is to visit one of the many dealers in your local area - don't travel miles. Used car dealers vary from small outfits operating out of a lock-up on a trading estate to your main franchised dealer. The former will be more likely to deal in the early models with a few more miles on the clock, while the main dealer will be the place to go for a nice late, low mileage motor. One thing both have in common is that you pay a premium for their service.

Used cars at your main dealer will be on offer for top money, sometimes well above top book. For this extra cash you'll get the pleasure of being able to deal with a nice salesman. A nice long test drive will be no problem, and all negotiations will take place in a spanking clean showroom over a few cups of free coffee. The car will be supplied freshly serviced and valeted, aftersales service is guaranteed, and you will have the peace-of-mind of a warranty. Check the terms of the warranty carefully - some cover you for sweet f.a. (many have excesses and maximum claim limits), and you may be obliged to have the vehicle serviced by the dealer during the warranty period.

The smaller used car outfits are a better option if funds are tight. The cars will be more realistically priced (but still above what you'd expect to pay privately/at auction) but the surroundings won't be quite as posh. You'll still be able to test drive the car and the car will (or should!) be supplied with a warranty. Again, check the warranty terms carefully. Although you will have some comeback, they're unlikely to be as obliging as a main dealer.

When buying from the smaller operations, it pays to treat them much as you would a private seller, and take nothing for granted. The nice man you're dealing with who desperately wants your money may not be quite as helpful when you bring the motor back in a month's time for some work under warranty.

Buying privately - one careful owner?

For most of us, this is the way to buy. The plus side is you'll pay a fair price for the car, but you may have to travel a few miles and look at a fair few vehicles before you find the one you're after. Even then, once you've parted with the cash, is the car all it seems, or does it have a hidden past? Buying privately is not without risks, but these risks can be minimised if you're careful.

Before phoning the owner for the first time, write down a list of questions to ask, so you find out as much as possible. Ask the exact model, colour, age and mileage. How many owners has it had, how

long has the present owner had it, and what has it been used for? What's the overall condition - any damage or faults at present, and why are they selling it? Is it taxed and MOT'd? These may seem obvious questions, but the owner's answers will give you a fair idea of what you're going to look at. A few extra minutes spent on the phone could just save you the time/expense of travelling a long way to see something which wasn't what it promised to be.

Buying privately, you get to meet the owner in person - this is a huge advantage over dealer-buying, as it can tell you masses about how the car's been treated. Everyone's nervous when buying a car, but don't ignore your "gut feeling" when you first see the car, or meet its owner. If you're not the world's greatest authority on cars, take someone knowledgeable along with you - preferably someone with experience of Saxos.

Always be sure to check the paperwork carefully, especially the vehicle registration document (V5). Are the owner's name and address correct - if not, why not? How many "former keepers" are showing? A lot of owners in a short space of time could point to trouble. The most important thing to do is to check that the VIN (Vehicle Identification Number) and engine number on the document match those on the vehicle. The VIN number appears on a plate riveted to the rear of the boot (peer in through the open tailgate); if there's any sign that this plate has been tampered with, walk away - the car could be stolen. The VIN number (also known as the chassis number) is also stamped onto the top of the engine

compartment bulkhead - again, if the number doesn't match, or looks like it's been tampered with, leave it alone. The engine number is located on the left-hand end of the front face of the engine block. This number can be difficult to spot, but keep looking until you find it - if the number's been ground off, or if there's anything suspicious about it, you could be buying trouble.

Is there any service history? If so, this is good, but study the service book carefully. Which garage has done the servicing? Is it a main dealer or a backstreet bodger? Do the mileages show a nice even progression, or are there huge gaps? Does it look as if the stamps are authentic or could this 'service history' have been created last week, to make the car look good? When was the last service, what exactly was carried out, and has the owner got receipts for any of this servicing work?

Check that the mileages and dates shown on the MOTs (where needed - cars less than 3 years old don't need one) follow a pattern indicating normal use, with no gaps in the dates, and no sudden drop in the mileage between MOTs (which might suggest the mileage has been 'clocked'). If you're presented with a sheaf of paperwork, it's worth going through it - maybe the car's had a history of problems, or maybe it's just had some pricey new parts fitted (like a clutch, starter motor or alternator, for instance).

Get a test drive to check the car drives and performs as expected, but also check the check simple things too, like making sure the windows and sunroof open and shut, and that all the doors and tailgate can be locked. Check all the basic electrical equipment too, as far as possible - lights, front and rear wipers, heated rear window, heater fan; it's amazing how often these things are taken for granted by buyers. Remember any genuine faults or defects you can find can be used as bargaining points when making the final deal. A word of warning, never buy a car in the dark, or when it's raining. If you do have to view any car in these conditions, agree not to hand over any money until you've seen it in daylight, and when the paintwork's dry (dull, faded paint, or metallic paint that's lost its lacquer, will appear to be shiny in the rain).

Everything as expected and the car's just what you want? It's time to start haggling. Never just agree to hand over the full advertised price for the car. Try a low offer to test the owner's

reaction (they can only say no!) then reluctantly increase the offer until you're both happy. Sorted! Before parting with any cash though, it may be worth considering the following:

a Run a check on the car through HPI or the AA. It'll cost you (usually about 30 quid) but could save a lot of hassle in future. They'll need the vehicle identification numbers at least - some can also verify the mileage, etc. For your money, they'll run the details of the car through their computer database, which contains records of all stolen vehicles, those which have been total losses (ie. written off after a serious accident) or have outstanding finance. They can confirm over the phone the car is straight, and you can proceed with the deal, safe in the knowledge you're not about to purchase a ringer. You later receive a nice certificate through the post with your car details on it. Running the check also gives you financial insurance, to the tune of about ten grand - if Plod turns up on your doorstep a month later, demanding you return your new car to its rightful owner, you get your cash back.

b If your understanding of a car's mechanical workings is a bit vague and you want a second opinion, it may be worth having the car inspected. The AA and RAC offer this service, but there may be other people in your area too - check in the Yellow Pages. This is a bit pricier than the HPI-type check, but will give you peace of mind and some comeback should things not be as expected. If you know a friendly garage, maybe they could be persuaded to check the car over for a small fee.

Auctions - not for the faint-hearted

This is not recommended for those of you with a nervous disposition. If you're not prepared to buy a car on the strength of a quick-look round and watching it being driven from one side of the auction ring to the other, then the auction is not the place for you. But if you like risks and believe that he who dares wins, a day out at the auctions could be a very financially-rewarding experience.

Auction sites are now spread fairly well across the country, and details can be found in the motoring press. Many of the larger sites will post details of the vehicles for sale on the internet the previous day, so you can check what's for sale before travelling. Even it you don't end up driving home in the vehicle of your dreams, a day out at the auctions is certainly an education. Believe me, once you've seen the sort of money vehicles change hands for at auction, you'll see just how much of a laugh used car dealers are having with the prices they charge on their forecourts.

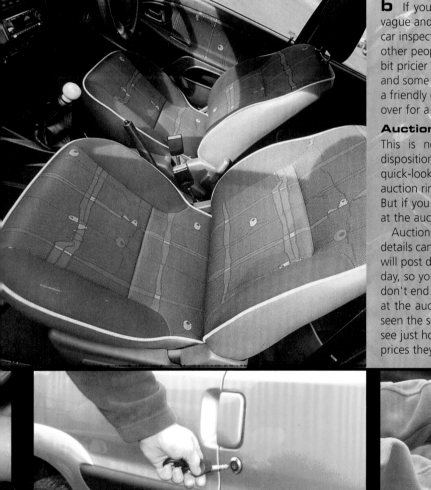

Model history

Like many small-car ranges in recent years, the number of "special edition" models offered in the Saxo's history has been enormous. The models listed are a representative selection - to have listed them all would've taken half the book! Don't pay over the odds for a special edition, unless it's genuinely got some extra kit you're interested in having - most are just the standard models with stickers and er... interesting seat trim!

Saxo "Phase I"

May 1996 (N reg)
3-door Hatchbacks launched: 1.1i LX and SX, 1.4i LX and VSX.

October 1996 (P reg)
1.5D diesel, 1.6i auto launched. 3 & 5-doors now available; LX models now rebadged as X.

January 1997
1.6i VTR (90 bhp) and 1.6i 16v VTS (120 bhp) launched. Sports seats, alloys, front fogs, arch extensions, electric windows, remote central locking. VTS also has passenger airbag, electric mirrors, ABS and leather-trimmed steering wheel.

June 1997
1.0i Mischief (3 dr, with Zest Yellow paint) and 1.1i Desire (3 dr) launched.
.

November 1997 (R reg)
Slight facelift, lightly-modified "smiley" grille and rear lights. Keypad immobiliser replaced by chip-in-key transponder type. 1.4 SX auto and Exclusive launched. VTR and VTS get blue dials.

March 1998
1.1i Spree launched.

May 1998
1.0i Scandal (3 dr), 1.0i Open Scandal (with full-length fabric sunroof), 1.0i Spree 2, 1.1i Expose (3 & 5 dr) launched.

October 1998 (S reg)
1.4i West Coast launched. Front fogs, sunroof, remote central locking.

May 1999 (T reg)
1.1i East Coast (3 dr) launched.

Saxo "Phase II"

October 1999 (V reg)
"Phase II" launched. Rounded bonnet, front "V" grille incorporated into bonnet, larger badge and clear-glass headlights. 1.0 litre First and 1.4 Exclusive models introduced. VTR and VTS now have white dials.

January 2000
1.4 Furio introduced, initially as a limited edition. Based on VTR but with 75 bhp engine, rear drum brakes, yellow gear knob, colour-coded seat belts.

June 2000 (W reg)
1.1 and 1.4 Desire and 1.1i Forte launched.

Insurance
A necessary evil

The way the insurance companies work out premiums and assess risks is a mystery to most of us. In general, the smaller the engine you have in your Saxo, the less you'll pay for insurance, so hopefully, a Saxo 1.1 X will be lots less to insure than a VTS. However, different companies can give wildly different quotes so it's vital to shop around. Always ring as many brokers and get as many quotes as you possibly can. A few extra minutes spent on the phone once a year may result in an extra few hundred quid in your back pocket.

With modified cars, insurance becomes even more of a problem. By modifying a car, you're making it more of a target for thieves (yes, ok, I know you know this). The point is, the insurance companies know this too, and they don't want to be paying out for the car, plus all the money you've spent on it, should it go missing. There is a temptation 'not to tell the insurance' about the mods you've made. Let's deal with this right now. Our experience has been that, while it can be painful, honesty is best. If they find out (and if you have a claim, they may well come and inspect the car) they won't pay out a penny. And if you do make a claim, very few insurers pay out for the modifications, so you get paid out, but based on a standard car. There are many specialist insurers who are more friendly towards fully-loaded cars, but even they won't actually cover the cost of replacement goodies.

Valuing your car

When your insurance pays out in the event of a total loss or write-off, they base their offer on the current market value of an identical standard model to yours. The only way you'll get more than the average amount is to prove your Saxo is in above-average nick (with photos) or that the mileage was especially low for the year.

With this in mind, don't bother over-valuing your Saxo in the hope you'll get more in the event of a claim - you won't! The only way to do this is to seek out an "agreed-value" deal, which you can usually only get on classic-car policies (with these, the car's value is agreed in advance between you, not worked out later by the company with you having no say in it). By over-valuing your Saxo, you could be increasing your premium without gaining any benefit.

Equally though, don't under-value, in the hope you'll get a reduction in premium. You won't, and if there's a total loss claim, you won't get any more than your under-valued amount, no matter how loudly you complain.

Work on what you paid for the car, backed up with the sort of prices you see for similar cars in the ads (or use a secondhand car price guide). Add no more than 10% for the sake of optimism, and that's it.

What type of cover?

For most of us, cost means there's only one option - TPF&T (third party, fire and theft). Fully-comp insurance is an unattainable dream for most people until they reach the "magic" age of 25, but what's the real story?

Third Party only

The most basic cover you can get. Basically covers you for damage to other people's cars or property, and for personal injury claims. Virtually no cover for your own stuff, beyond what you get if you take the optional "legal protection" cover.

Third Party, Fire and Theft

As above, with cover for fire and theft, of course! Better, but not much better. This is really only cover in the event of a "total loss", if your car goes missing or goes up in smoke. Still no cover for your car if you stack it into a tree, or if someone breaks in and pinches your stereo.

Fully-comprehensive

In theory, covers you for any loss or damage. Will cover the cost of repairing or replacing your car regardless of whether it was your fault or not. With a fully-comp policy, you can "protect" your no-claims bonus for a small fee so you don't automatically lose those hard-earned years' worth of discount if you prang it All this extra cover costs more, but is often a better bet in the long run.

Your car, or your Dad's?

Don't pretend your Saxo belongs to your Dad, and get him to insure it, with you as a named driver. Insurance companies are not stupid. They know that your Dad isn't likely to be running around in a modified car, and they treat any "named driver" application with great suspicion in these cases. This dubious practice also does you no favours in future years. All the time you're living the lie, you're not building up any no-claims bonus of your own.

Not telling the insurance company the whole truth gets a little tricky when you have to make a claim. You may think your insurance company is there for your benefit, but they're a business like any other, and their main aim in life is to make money. If the insurance assessor comes around to check your bent/burnt/stolen-and-recovered "standard" Saxo, and finds he's looking at a vehicle fitted with alloys/bodykit/modified interior, he's not going to turn a blind eye.

Limit your premium

When you phone for a quote your fate is pretty much sealed, but there are a few things you can do to help lower the premium.

Golden Rule Number One

If in doubt, declare everything. Insurance companies are legally entitled to dispute any claim if the car is found to be non-standard in any way.

Golden Rule Number Two

Before modifying the car, ring your insurers, and ask them how it will affect things.

Fit an approved alarm or immobiliser

In general, any alarm or immobiliser with a Thatcham rating should be recognised by any insurance company, but it pays to check before fitting. In some cases, the discounts offered are not that great any more - but an alarm is still a nice way to get peace of mind.

Avoid speed cameras and The Law

Yes, okay, easier said than done! One SP30 isn't usually too bad, but much more and you'll pay for it, so go easy.

Make yourself the only driver

Pretty self-explanatory. The more people who drive your car, the greater the risk to the company. If you've built up 2 years' worth of no-claims, but your partner hasn't, putting them on your insurance will bump it up, due to their relative inexperience.

Build up your no-claims bonus

You'll only do this by owning and insuring a car in your own name, and then not making any claims. Simple really. Each claim free year you have will aid lowering how much you pay out.

Hang onto your no-claims bonus

Obviously, the less you claim, the less your insurance will cost. If something happens to your car, don't be in too big a hurry to make a claim before you've thought it all through. How much will it cost to fix? How much is your excess? If you can afford not to claim, then don't do it.

Limit your mileage

Most companies offer a discount if you only cover a small annual mileage. To get any meaningful reduction, the mileage has to be less than 10,000 per year. Don't try and pretend you only do 3000 if it's nearer 20,000. Few companies ever ask what the car's current mileage is - so how are they gonna know if you've gone over your self-imposed limit? But if they do find out you could be in trouble.

Get a garage

If you have access to a garage, use it. Iinsurers love a car to be locked away safe and sound at night.

Insurance-friendly mods?

So - what do insurance companies like and dislike, as far as mods go? No two companies will have the same outlook, and your own circumstances will play a big part too.

Engine mods

"Mild" mods, such as induction kits and exhausts don't often change premiums, but just the merest mention of "chipping" can make many companies load the premium, or even completely refuse to offer cover. With complete engine transplants, you may be required to give an engineer's report on the mods before they'll grant cover.

Interior mods

As with bodykits, unless you go absolutely mental it really shouldn't make a difference, but make sure you tell your insurers all the same.

Body mods

Even a tiny rear spoiler can be classed as a "bodykit" (yes, it's daft, but that's how it is). Anything which alters the exterior appearance should be declared. As long as the mods aren't too radical, the jump in premium should be fairly small. If anything at all.

Lights

As they're safety-related, you'll probably get asked for lots of details, but as long as you've kept it sensible (and legal) you'll be fine.

Security

Make sure you mention all security stuff - alarms, immobilisers (including mechanical devices), and locking wheel nuts. Don't tell them you've got a Cat 1 if your alarm really came from Argos, and don't tell them you garage the car at night if it's stuck out in the road; if they find out, you're on your own.

Suspension

Average suspension drops of 30-40mm are fine, go much lower and they may charge you more.

Wheels

The specialist insurers won't mind you having a nice set of alloys, but just about every other insurer will load the premium, sadly. Make sure you fit locking wheel bolts.

Brakes

Uprating standard sized discs, maybe with grooved or drilled discs seldom affects the insurance, but some get a bit twitchy when you start fitting bigger discs and replacement calipers.

Security

It's a sad fact, but making your car attractive to the opposite sex also tends to attract attention of a less-welcome kind from less-than-human low-lifes.

Avoiding trouble

Now come on - you're modifying your car to look cool and to be seen in. Not a problem - but be careful where you choose to show your car off, and who to. Be especially discreet, the nearer you get to home - turn your system down before you get near home, for instance, or you'll draw unwelcome attention to where that car with the loud stereo's parked at night.

If you're going out, think about where you're parking - somewhere well-lit and reasonably well-populated is the best bet.

Hands up, who doesn't lock their car when they get petrol? Your insurance company has a term for this, and it's "contributory negligence". In English, this means you won't get a penny if your car goes missing when you haven't locked it.

If you're lucky enough to have a garage, use it and fit extra security to the garage door.

Always use all the security you have, whenever you leave the car, even if it's a bit of a chore fitting a steering lock, just do it.

A word about your stereo

From the moment you bolt on those nice alloys, it's taken as read that you've also got stereo gear that's worth nicking - and the thieves know it. All the discreet installation in the world isn't going to deter them from finding out what's inside that nice motor.

If you have a CD player, don't leave discs or empty CD cases lying around inside the car. 6x9s on the rear shelf are also very inviting to thieves, and very easy to steal. When you're fitting your system, give some thought to the clues you could accidentally leave in plain view. Oxygen-free speaker cable is great stuff, but it's also a bit bright against dark carpets, and is all the clue necessary that you're serious about your speakers.

Most modern sets are face-off or MASK, so if they've got security features like this, use them - take your faceplate off when you leave the car, and take it with you rather than leaving it in the door pocket or glovebox (the first places a thief will look).

Things that go beep in the night

Don't skimp on an alarm, it may never even be put to the test, but if it is, you'll be glad you spent wisely …

The simplest first step to car security is to fake it. It's obviously risky if the thief calls your bluff, but if you really can't afford an alarm just an LED is cheap to buy and easy to fit, and can be rigged to a discreet switch inside the car (we show you how, later on).

Don't overlook the value of so-called "manual" immobilisers, such as steering wheel locks. These are a worthwhile deterrent - a thief not specifically after your car (and yours alone) may move on to an easier target. Some of the items offered may be "Sold Secure" or Thatcham Cat 3, accolades well worth checking out, as it means they've withstood a full-on brute force attack for a useful length of time.

The only way to combat the more determined thief is to go for a well-specified and intelligently-installed alarm. Immobilisers alone have their place, but a pro-fitted immobiliser alone won't stop someone pinching your wheels, or breaking in for the stereo gear.

Finally, one other scam which you might fall victim to. If you find that your alarm is suddenly going off a lot at night, when previously it had been well-behaved, don't ignore the problem. It's an old trick for a thief to deliberately set off your alarm several times, each time hiding when you come out to investigate, then to wait until the fifth or sixth time when you don't reset, leaving him a clear run. If your alarm does keep false-alarming without outside assistance, find out the cause quickly, or your neighbours will quickly become "deaf" to it.

Thatcham categories and meanings:

1 **Cat 1.** For alarms and electronic immobilisers.

2 **Cat 2.** For electronic immobilisers only.

3 **Cat 2-1.** Electronic immobilisers which can be upgraded to Cat 1 alarms later.

4 **Cat 3.** Mechanical immobilisers, eg. snap-off steering wheels, locking wheel bolts, window film, steering wheel locks/covers.

5 **Q-class.** Tracking devices.

Other alarm features

Two-stage anti-shock - means that the alarm shouldn't go off, just because the neighbour's cat jumps on your car roof, or because Little Johnny punts his football into your car. Alarm will only sound after a major shock, or after repeated shocks are detected.

Anti-tilt - detects any attempt to lift or jack up the car, preventing any attempt to pinch alloys. Very unpopular with thieves, as it makes the alarm very sensitive (much more so than anti-shock). Alarm may sound if car is parked outside in windy conditions (but not if your suspension's rock-hard!).

Anti-hijack - immobiliser with built-in delay. If your motor gets hijacked, the neanderthals responsible will only get so far down the road before the engine cuts out.

Rolling code - reduces the chance of your alarm remote control signal from being "grabbed" by special electronic equipment.

Total closure - module which connects to electric windows or sunroof and central locking, which closes all items when alarm is set.

Pager control - yes, really - your alarm can be set to send a message to your pager (why not your mobile?) if your car gets tampered with.

Current-sensing disable - very useful feature on some cars which have a cooling fan which can cut in after the ignition is switched off. Without this feature, your alarm will be triggered every time you leave it parked after a long run - very annoying.

Volumetric-sensing disable - basically allows you to manually disable the interior ultrasonics, leaving the rest of the alarm features active. Useful if you want to leave the sunroof open in hot weather - if a fly gets in the car, the alarm would otherwise be going off constantly.

Talking alarms - no, please, please no. Very annoying, and all that'll happen is you'll attract crowds of kids daring each other to set it off again. Unfortunately, these are becoming more popular, with some offering the facility to record your own message.

The knowledge

What people often fail to realise (at least, until it happens to them) is the level of violence and destruction which thieves will employ to get your stuff - this goes way beyond breaking a window.

It comes as a major shock to most people when they discover the serious kinds of tools (weapons) at many professional thieves' disposal, and how brutally your lovingly-polished car will be attacked. Many people think, for instance, that it's their whole car they're after, whereas it's really only the parts they want, and they don't care how they get them (this means that these parts are still attractive, even when fitted to a basic car which has yet to be fully modded). Obviously, taking the whole car then gives the option of hiding it to strip at leisure, but it won't always be the option chosen, and you could wake up one morning to a well-mangled wreck outside.

Attack 1 The first option to any thief is to smash glass - typically, the toughened-glass side windows, which will shatter, unlike the windscreen. Unfortunately for the thief, this makes a loud noise (not good), but is a quick and easy way in. The reason for taking this approach is that a basic car alarm will only go off if the doors are opened (voltage-drop alarm) - provided the doors aren't opened, the alarm won't go off.

Response 1 A more sophisticated alarm will feature shock sensing (which will be set off by the impact on the glass), and better still, ultrasonic sensing, which will be triggered by the brick coming in through the broken window.

Response 2 This kind of attack can also be stopped by applying security film to the inside of the glass, which holds it all together and prevents easy entry.

Attack 2 An alternative to smashing the glass is to pry open the door using a crowbar - this attack involves literally folding open the door's window frame by prising from the top corner. The glass will still shatter, but as long as the door stays shut, a voltage-drop alarm won't be triggered.

Response This method might not be defeated by a shock-sensing alarm, but an ultrasonic unit would pick it up.

Incidentally, another bonus with ultrasonic alarms is that the sensors are visible from outside - and act as a deterrent.

Attack 3 The next line of attack is to disable the alarm. The commonest way to kill the alarm is either to cut the wiring to the alarm itself, or to disconnect the battery after taking a crowbar to your bonnet.

Response 1 If your alarm has extra pin-switches, be sure to fit one to the bonnet, and fit it in the bonnet channel next the battery, so that it'll set off the alarm if the bonnet is prised up. Also make sure that the wire to the pin-switch cannot be cut easily though a partly-open bonnet.

Response 2 Make sure that the alarm module is well-hidden, and cannot be got at from underneath the car.

Response 3 Make the alarm power supply connection somewhere less obvious than directly at the battery terminal - any thief who knows his stuff will immediately cut any "spare" red wires at the battery. Try taking power from the fusebox, or if you must source it under the bonnet, trace the large red battery lead to the starter motor connections, and tap into the power there.

Response 4 Always disguise the new alarm wiring, by using black insulating tape to wrap it to the existing wiring loom. Tidying up in this way also helps to ensure the wires can't get trapped, cut, melted, or accidentally ripped out - any of which could leave you with an alarm siren which won't switch off, or an immobiliser you can't disable.

Response 5 An alarm which has a "battery back-up" facility is best. Even if he's successfully crow-barred your bonnet and snipped the battery connections, the alarm will still go off, powered by a separate battery of its own. A Cat 1 alarm has to have battery back-up.

Fitting
a basic
LED

All you need for this is a permanent live feed, an earth, a switch if you want to be able to turn it on/off, and the flashing LED itself (very cheap, from any car accessory shop).

An LED draws very little current, so tap into almost any live feed you fancy. If you've wired in your ICE, take a live feed from the permanent (radio memory supply) wire at the back of your head unit, or go into fusebox with your test light. An earth can easily be tapped again from your head unit, or you can make one almost anywhere on the metal body of the car - drill a small hole, fit a self-tapping screw, then wrap the bared end of wire around and tighten it.

The best place to mount an LED is into one of the blank switches the makers love fitting. The blank switch is pried out, and a hole can then be drilled to take the LED (which comes in a separate little holder). Feed the LED wiring down behind the dashboard to where you've tapped your live and earth, taking care not to trap it anywhere, nor to accidentally wrap it around any moving parts.

Connect your live to the LED red wire, then rig your earth to one side of the switch, and connect the LED black wire to the other switch terminal. You should now have a switchable LED. Tidy up the wiring, and mount the switch somewhere discreet, but where you can still get at it. Switch on when you leave the car, and it looks as if you've got some sort of alarm - better than nothing!

Wiring
basics

If you were thinking of taking an alarm live supply direct from the battery - don't. It's better to trace the red lead down to the starter motor, and tap in there.

If a thief manages to get past your bonnet switch, his first thought will be to cut every additional live feed at the battery - of course, if he cuts all the battery leads, you're stuffed (without a battery back-up alarm), but at least you tried…

With your wires identified, how to tap into them?

The best options are:

Soldering - avoids cutting through your chosen wire - strip away a short section of insulation, wrap your new wire around the bared section, then apply solder to secure it. If you're a bit new to soldering, practice on a few offcuts of wire first.

Bullet connectors - cut and strip the end of your chosen wire, wrap your new one to it, push both into one half of the bullet. Connect the other end of your victim wire to the other bullet, and connect together. Always use the "female" half on any live feed - it'll be safer if you disconnect it than a male bullet, which could touch bare metal and send your motor up in smoke.

Block connectors - so easy to use. Just remember that the wires can come adrift if the screws aren't really tight, and don't get too ambitious about how many wires you can stuff in one hole (block connectors, like bullets, are available in several sizes).
Steer clear of connectors like the one below – they're convenient but can give rise to problems.

With any of these options, always insulate around your connection - especially when soldering, or you'll be leaving bare metal exposed. Remember that you'll probably be shoving all the wires up into the dark recesses of the under-dash area - by the time the wires are nice and kinked/squashed together, that tiny bit of protruding wire might just touch that bit of metal bodywork, and cause a fire…

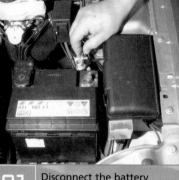

Alarm fitting

The alarm we've chosen to fit is a Texalarm 9471.G2 from our local Citroën dealer, which plugs in to the existing immobiliser and brings the protection to Thatcham Cat 1. Pretty useful. This alarm can be fitted to other models, with the use of a different wiring harness. Luckily, we can use the harness which plugs straight in to the existing system.

The following procedure only applies to fitting the above alarm, but most of the principles remain the same whatever you're fitting. Like reading the instructions provided, first, and during the fitting procedure if you get stuck.

01 Disconnect the battery negative lead, and move the lead away from the battery. Might screw up your stereo settings, but it's better than having sparks flying and your new alarm going mental the minute it's rigged up.

06 Insert one of the grey wires into the Raychem connector, and from the other end insert the red alarm wire and the other grey wire.

07 Heat the solder with a soldering iron until it melts and fixes the wires together.

08 Pull over the black rubber cover and carefully heat it, using the soldering iron, until it shrinks and seals the connector.

09 Repeat the above procedure (paragraphs 4 to 8) using the orange alarm wire and the green vehicle wire (CH01B stamped on it). Reconnect the black connector.

02 Decide where you're going to mount the alarm/siren. Choose somewhere not easily reached from underneath. Will the wiring supplied with the alarm reach to the fusebox? It's also best to pick a location away from where you'll be topping up washers, oil or coolant. We chose to fit the alarm on the passenger side inner wing, behind the headlight. There are two holes already drilled, which fit the siren bracket mounting holes a treat. Secure the siren to the bracket.

Now it's time to earth the system. Best place, and easiest to get to , is the earthing point behind the passenger side footwell kick panel. Carefully unclip the carpet and pull it to one side - the earthing point lies in front of you.

03 Next, find the wiring connector (large, black and round) underneath the dashboard - you need a long flexible neck for this - and disconnect it by unscrewing it.

04 Cut the grey vehicle wire (BH05C stamped on it). This has now got to be connected to the red alarm wire. We used Raychem connectors.

05 Place the black rubber connector cover over one of the wires, and push to one side. This will be used later to cover and seal the complete connector.

10

11 Attach the alarm wiring eyelet to the earthing point, and do up the bolt.

12 Still working in the footwell, remove the Torx screw and take out the front door switch.

13 Remove the large rubber grommet, and thread the white/black alarm wire through the grommet's centre hole.

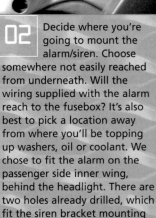

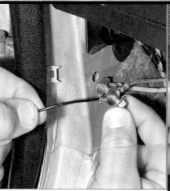

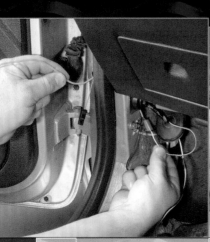

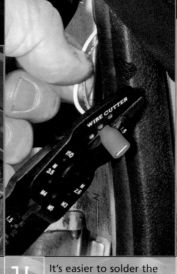

14 Thread a spare piece of wire through the hole for the door switch and down through the hole which the grommet came out of. Attach the white/black wire (alarm wire) to the spare piece of wire with some tape, and pull the wiring back up through the door switch hole.

15 You then need to attach the alarm wire to the spare terminal on the back of the door switch. It fits the terminal, but the switch may not go back in place.

16 It's easier to solder the door switch wiring and the alarm wire together, and stick a new connector on the end.

17 Refit the door switch and refit the rubber grommet.

Now with the LED in your hand, pull back the white cover from the LED. Remove the LED from its black surround and thread the LED through the blanking panel.

22

Replace the LED black surround and secure the LED to the blanking panel.

23

Fit the white LED cover to the rear of the LED.

24

Now connect the LED to the harness connector which you threaded through earlier . . .

25

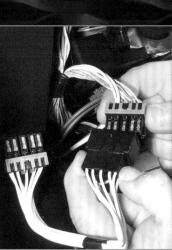

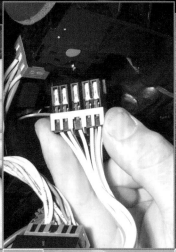

18 Remove the two Torx screws securing the steering column cowling (this picture was taken when fitting our Momo wheel - you don't have to take off the steering wheel). Run the alarm harness across the back of the dashboard, so you can fit the (black) alarm harness connections to the indicator switch. Unclip the indicator multi-plug connector from the car . . .

19 . . . then plug it into the alarm harness connector

20 Plug the alarm harness connector into the socket where the car indicator multiplug connector came from. Tuck all the wiring away, and refit the cowling.

21 To fit the LED on to the dashboard, carefully prise out one of the blank switch panels. Retrieve the wiring and its connector for the LED, and thread the connector through the blanking panel hole. Using an 8 mm drill bit, carefully drill a hole through the centre of the blank switch panel.

Working in the engine compartment, locate the grommet on the bulkhead which will enable you to pass the wiring through to the passenger footwell. Using a piece of stiff wire, pass it through the bulkhead and attach the wiring for the siren/bonnet switch.

26 . . . then refit the blanking panel back onto the dashboard.

27 To connect up the boot light, thread the white/green alarm wire down the passenger side of the car so that it reappears behind the boot light. This is fairly easy - most of the trim panels

unclip, apart from the section that the boot light is fitted to (two Torx screws). Remove the rear seat cushion. Connect the alarm wire to the car wire labelled 319 (pin 2 - our wire was orange, but the colour may vary).

28 Pull the wiring through into the passenger footwell.

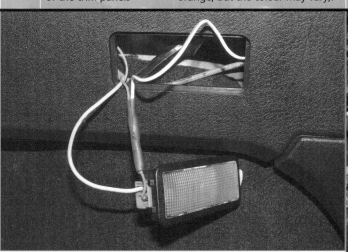

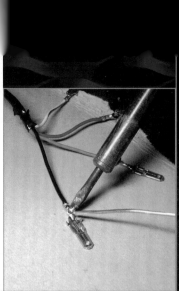

29 Solder each wire to the supplied spade terminals (one each) and fit them into the white terminal block in the following order. Note: The wire colours listed are the ones on our Saxo - yours may be different. The "male" plug is the list of wires you have to attach spades to, and the "female" is the one each wire terminal plugs into.

These are the connections on our Saxo -

Male plug	**Female plug**
Pin 1 No wire	Pin 1 No wire
Pin 2 Red	Pin 2 Red
Pin 3 Black	Pin 3 Black
Pin 4 Blue/White	Pin 4 White
Pin 5 Blue	Pin 5
	Blue/Yellow

30 Now clip the bonnet switch on to the bonnet lock . . .

31 . . . and connect the bonnet switch connector to the alarm wiring harness.

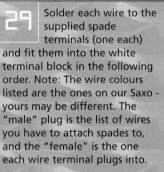

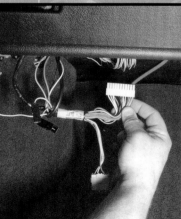

. . . plug the original 9-way connector into one, and the other into the central locking control unit.

36

You now have to fit the alarm control unit in a suitable place. We decided to fit it to the rear of the glovebox.

37

We made a template of the mounting holes on the control unit, and drilled some holes in the back of the glovebox. Discreet but accessible!

38

Connect the alarm wiring harness to the alarm control unit.

39

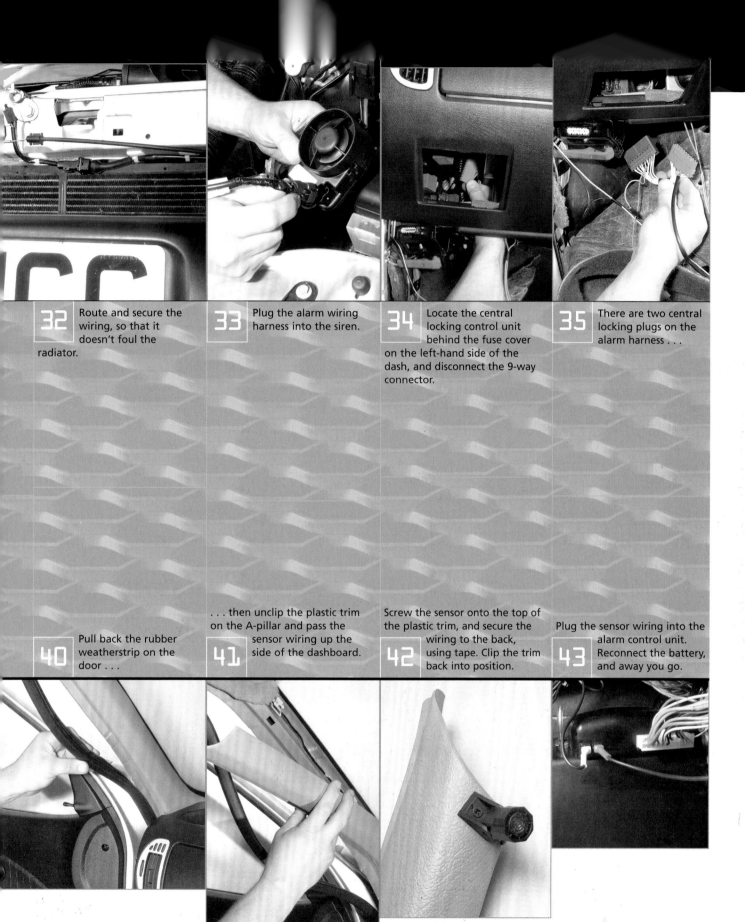

32 Route and secure the wiring, so that it doesn't foul the radiator.

33 Plug the alarm wiring harness into the siren.

34 Locate the central locking control unit behind the fuse cover on the left-hand side of the dash, and disconnect the 9-way connector.

35 There are two central locking plugs on the alarm harness . . .

40 Pull back the rubber weatherstrip on the door . . .

41 . . . then unclip the plastic trim on the A-pillar and pass the sensor wiring up the side of the dashboard.

42 Screw the sensor onto the top of the plastic trim, and secure the wiring to the back, using tape. Clip the trim back into position.

43 Plug the sensor wiring into the alarm control unit. Reconnect the battery, and away you go.

Body
styling

If you're planning a major body job, you've
probably already got some good ideas about how
you want your Saxo to look, from 'Max Power' or
something similar, or maybe from a friend's car.

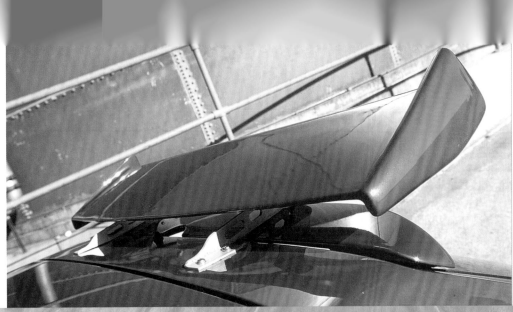

Nothing girly about this spoiler - this is one Saxo that ain't taking off!

While it can be good to have a target car to aim for, if you're just starting out on the road towards a fully-loaded car, you probably don't want (or can't quite afford) to go 'all the way' all at once. If you're new to the world of modifying, it's a good idea to start with smaller jobs, and work up to the full body kit gradually, as your skills increase; spending loads on a body kit is a pretty dumb idea if you then make a mess of fitting it! There's plenty of small ways to improve the look of your Saxo, which don't cost much, and which are simple enough to fit; start with some of these before you go too mad!

Take it easy and break less

One golden rule with any body mods is to plan what you're going to do, and don't rush it. It's better that the car looks a bit stupid for a week (because you couldn't get something finished) than to rush a job and have the car look stupid forever.

Try and think the jobs through - don't just say to yourself: "Right. Now I'm going to fit those new mirrors!" - read through the instructions, then see what we say, and plan each stage. Have you got all the tools, screws or whatever before you start, or will you have to break off halfway through? If you get stuck, is there someone you can get to help, or have they gone off for the weekend? Above all, if something goes wrong - don't panic - a calm approach will prove to be a huge bonus (that job doesn't have to be done today, does it?).

If a piece of trim won't come off, don't force it. If something feels like it's going to break, it probably will - stop and consider whether to go on and break it, or try another approach. Some things either never come off as easily as you think, or else have already been off so many times that they break or won't fit back on properly. While we'd all like to do a perfect job every time, working on a car will, sooner or later, teach you the fine art of 'bodging' (finding valid alternative ways of fixing things!). Bodging is fine (if you've no choice) with interior and exterior trim, but make sure there are no safety implications - gluing an exterior mirror on might just about work with the car stood still, but it's going to fall off half a mile down the road, isn't it? Any Tips 'n' Tricks we give in our procedures are things we've tried ourselves, which we know will work. Also, don't assume that you'll have to bodge something back on, every time - if a trim clip breaks when you take something off, it might be easier and cheaper than you think to simply go to your Citroën dealer, and buy a new clip.

Is it a boot-scraper, or a wicked rear diffuser?

One devilishly saucy set of mirrors could be going on your Saxo - read on...

Meshed grille anyone?

One of the easiest mods to do on your Saxo is to mesh the grille.
It's straightforward, and looks great. As with everything else in
the world of modifying, grille fashions change quickly -
hopefully, though, this will at least give you some good ideas,
and a helping hand to what's involved in fitting.

There are many different styles you can achieve, you can spray up
the original grille, or just fit some mesh behind the original grille,
it's up to you! Especially on "Phase I" Saxos, the Citroën badge is
often first to go but this does leave a bit of a gaping hole.
Headlight makers Morette also do a ready-made mesh grille for
"Phase I" models.

Plenty of mesh styles to choose from, but for the Saxo, we felt
the classic diamond mesh was best suited. You may feel differently.
But we don't care.

Meshing the grille

01   Unscrew and unclip the grille from the bonnet.

02   Cut off the melted retaining lugs from the back of the grille, and separate the two parts.

03   Cut out the area of the grille that you don't want, but take care not to cut off the screw holes. (We used a new grille, which is much easier from the start - hence the change in colour.)

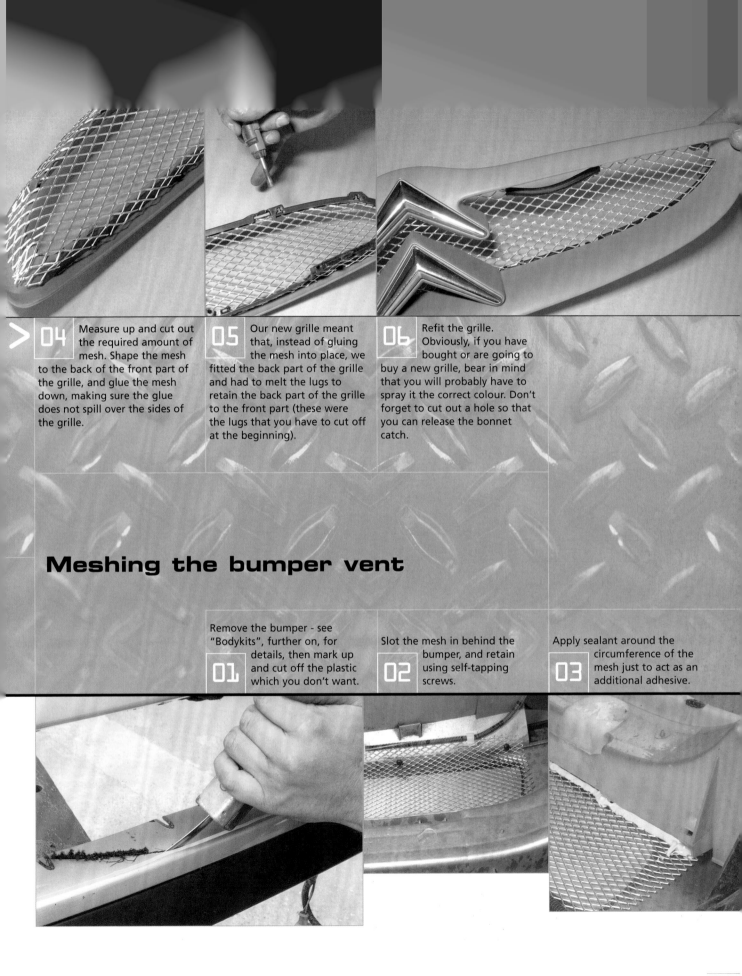

04 Measure up and cut out the required amount of mesh. Shape the mesh to the back of the front part of the grille, and glue the mesh down, making sure the glue does not spill over the sides of the grille.

05 Our new grille meant that, instead of gluing the mesh into place, we fitted the back part of the grille and had to melt the lugs to retain the back part of the grille to the front part (these were the lugs that you have to cut off at the beginning).

06 Refit the grille. Obviously, if you have bought or are going to buy a new grille, bear in mind that you will probably have to spray it the correct colour. Don't forget to cut out a hole so that you can release the bonnet catch.

Meshing the bumper vent

01 Remove the bumper - see "Bodykits", further on, for details, then mark up and cut off the plastic which you don't want.

02 Slot the mesh in behind the bumper, and retain using self-tapping screws.

03 Apply sealant around the circumference of the mesh just to act as an additional adhesive.

Mirror Mirror

Another simple-to-fit essential accessory, the DTM- or M3-style door mirror is well-established on the modified car circuit. Most mirrors are supplied in either carbon-look, or in black for spraying if desired.

Cheapest option is the "universal-fit" mirror. Bear in mind that "universal-fit" does not mean "easy-fit", and almost always means a lot of work is involved cutting and shaping to suit. If you can afford it, go for mirrors which are specifically designed for your Saxo - they'll be much easier to fit, and chances are, they'll end up looking better too.

01 Prise the mirror trim plate from the inner edge of the door. On manually-operated mirrors, remove the clamp screw securing the adjuster knob to the trim plate, and withdraw the trim plate; pull the adjuster grommet from the door.

02 You next need to remove the door trim panel (check out the "Interiors" section for that). Remove the three mirror securing screws. On electric mirrors, disconnect wiring plugs. Withdraw the mirror, complete with the adjuster mechanism and grommet (if applicable).

03 Spray up your new mirrors before finally fitting in place - use the info in "Painting your Saxo" if necessary. Don't be in too big a hurry - let the paint dry fully before handling. Place the mirror into position and screw into place. You may find that you might need to use washers to assist the positioning. Refit the door trim.

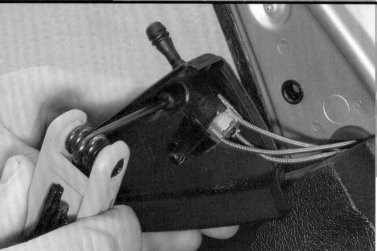

Aero
filler cap

The humble fuel filler flap. Not much to it, really - just a cap that unclips. We decided to replace the boring one with a Dimma Evo.

01 Insert the key and remove the fuel cap. Carefully unclip the plastic surround.

02 Lock the cap back into the filler neck. Remove the key and remove the plastic surround.

 Attention! *Fuel vapour is explosive. No smoking or naked lights anywhere near the open fuel filler, please.*

03 Place and clip on the new surround.

Beesting
aerial

A good, and simple mod is the 'Beesting' aerial, made popular by the VW Golf. The Saxo does come with Citroën's variation on the beesting, but there are more attractive alternatives such as this alloy example.

Fitting is simple - all you have to do is unscrew the old aerial and screw on the new one.

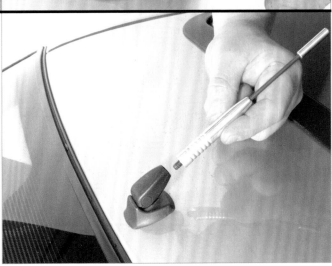

We took off our tailgate badges when we were smoothing our rear end, a bit further on.

De-badging

If you've bought a basic Saxo, it's understandable that you might not want to declare this fact loudly from the rear end of your car. Badges also clutter up the otherwise clean lines.

De-badging and general smoothing can be carried out on any Saxo. De-badging involves heating and prising off the old badges as carefully as possible, welding or filling the resulting holes with filler, and re-touching the paint. While the filler's out, why not try de-seaming, which involves filling over any welded joints in the bodywork.

The badges on the door rubbing strips (VTR badges in our case) can be peeled off, but take your time doing this. Try not to mark the plastic trim. You can purchase badges from Citroën if you wish. We chose VTS badges to replace our VTR badges. All you need is some decent glue that doesn't eat into plastic, and stick them on. Some badges come ready-glued.

Sun strip

When it comes to screen strips there are two options to make your car look (and maybe even feel) cooler:

a The sunvisor, a screen tint band inside the screen. As this fits inside, there's a problem straight away - the interior mirror. The Saxo mirror is bonded to the screen, and it seriously gets in the way when trying to fit a wet and sticky strip of plastic around it.

b The sunstrip, which is opaque vinyl, colour-matched to the car, fits to the outside of the screen.

01 This is stuck to the outside, so do a good job of cleaning - any dirt stuck under the strip will ruin the effect.

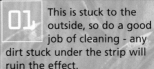

02 Spray the screen with water, then lay the strip on top, with the protective film part touching the glass.

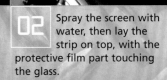

Trim the strip into place, tucking it under the windscreen rubber. As you work around, try to make a tidy job of the corners by cutting in one movement, rather than lots of little nicks. When trimming an opaque strip like this, it's not easy to judge where the rubber ends, so watch out or you'll end up trimming the rubber.

03 Get a mate to help check the strip's level - use the top corners of the windscreen rubber as a guide for measuring from.

04 Squeegee the strip down onto the screen, working it into the corners as best you can for now.

05 Spray and squeegee out all the bubbles and creases.

Tricks 'n' tips

Don't be in too much of a hurry to trim the strip dead accurately to the windscreen rubber - there is a better way. Use a small screwdriver to gently lift the edge of the windscreen rubber off the glass, then tuck the edge of the sunstrip underneath. If you haven't been too brutal with the knife (and made the rubber edge itself ragged), you should have a neat result with minimal effort. Sweet!

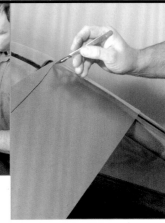

Travelling incognito

As with so much in modifying, window tinting is a matter of personal taste - it can look right with the right car and colour, but it doesn't suit everybody.

There's more than a little styling element to tinting, now that you can buy "reflex film", which incorporates a layer of precious metal (which reduces UV light and reflects heat from the sun), and is available in various wild colours, to complement or contrast your car's paint job. Only downside is - it's not legal to run it on the road, since many are advertised as "for show cars only" (see "Legal Eagle").

Kits fall into two main groups - one where you get a roll of film, which you then cut to shape, or a pre-cut kit where the film pieces are supplied to suit your car. In theory, the second option is better, but it leaves little margin for error - if you muck up fitting one of the supplied sections, you'll have to buy another complete kit. The roll-of-film kit may leave enough over for a few false starts … check when buying how many windows you'll be able to do.

All the work must be done with scrupulous cleanliness, as any muck or stray bits of trimmed-off film will ruin the effect. The other problem is that getting rid of air bubbles and creases can take time. This is another test of patience, because if, as the instructions say, you've used plenty of spray, it will take a while to dry out and stick… just don't panic!

Legal eagle

The law on window tinting currently is that there must be no more than a 25% reduction in light transmission through windscreens, and a limit of 30% reduction on all other glass. Yes, yes, all very well, but how the heck do you MEASURE light reduction? Also, consider that many cars come with tinted glass as standard - so can you fit a tinting kit on top and still be legal? Hard to know what line to take, if you're stopped by the police - try and choose a tinting kit which is EC-approved (ask before you buy, and if you think it could be a serious issue, get a letter from the company to support the legality of the kit, to use in your defence). Some police forces now take this seriously enough to have portable test equipment they can use at the roadside - if your car fails, it's an on-the-spot fine.

Tinting windows

Don't pick a windy day to do this - there'll be more dust in the air, and it'll be a nightmare trying to stop the film flapping and folding onto itself while you're working. Applying window tint is best done on a warm day (or in a warm garage - if there is such a thing), because the adhesive will begin to dry sooner. Don't try tinting when it's starting to get dark! It's a good idea to have a mate to help out with this job.

01 Get the window being tinted really clean, inside and out. Don't use glass cleaners (or any other product) containing ammonia or vinegar, since both these will react with the film or its adhesive, and muck it up. It's also worth cleaning the working area around the window, because it's easy for stray dirt to attach itself to the film - by the time you've noticed it, it could be too late. On door windows, wind them down slightly, to clean all of the top edge, then close them tight to fit the film.

02 When doing a door window, it's a good idea to remove the door trim panel - there'll be a fair bit of water about, for a start, and removing the panel will give you better access to the lower edge of the glass (refer to "Interiors" for door trim panel removal).

If you've got a pre-cut kit, you can probably ignore this bit - it's cutting to size. Before you even unroll the film, take note - handle it carefully. If you crease it, you won't get the creases out. Hold the roll of film up to the outside of the glass, and cut off a piece just slightly longer than the window. Tape it in place at the top.

03

The next step is to establish which way up the film is - ie which is the tint, and which is the protective (clear) film. Take one corner of your cut piece, and apply a small bit of really sticky tape to both sides - use the tape to pull the films

04

apart, just at one corner. Once apart, the identity of the films will be obvious. With our roll, the clear film was on the outside of the roll. The tinted film should be against the glass at this stage (clear side facing you).

Using scissors (not a knife, or you'll damage your paint or the window rubber), trim round the outside of the window (for now, follow the outside of the window rubber). You should end up with a window-shaped piece of film, just bigger than the glass.

05

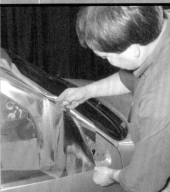

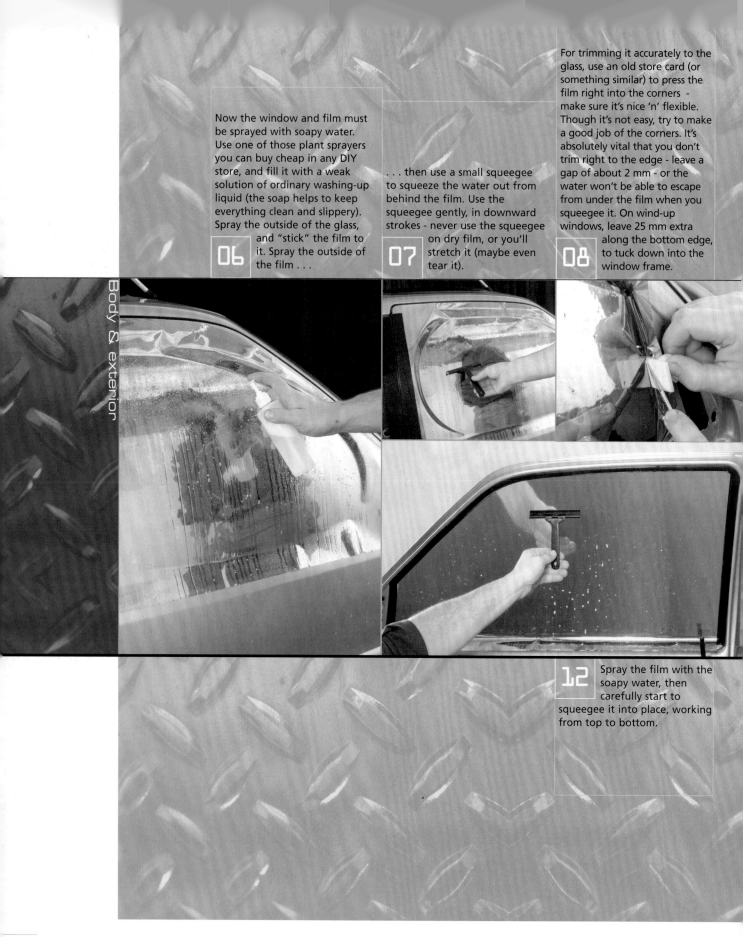

Now the window and film must be sprayed with soapy water. Use one of those plant sprayers you can buy cheap in any DIY store, and fill it with a weak solution of ordinary washing-up liquid (the soap helps to keep everything clean and slippery). Spray the outside of the glass, and "stick" the film to it. Spray the outside of the film . . .

06

. . . then use a small squeegee to squeeze the water out from behind the film. Use the squeegee gently, in downward strokes - never use the squeegee on dry film, or you'll stretch it (maybe even tear it).

07

For trimming it accurately to the glass, use an old store card (or something similar) to press the film right into the corners - make sure it's nice 'n' flexible. Though it's not easy, try to make a good job of the corners. It's absolutely vital that you don't trim right to the edge - leave a gap of about 2 mm - or the water won't be able to escape from under the film when you squeegee it. On wind-up windows, leave 25 mm extra along the bottom edge, to tuck down into the window frame.

08

12 Spray the film with the soapy water, then carefully start to squeegee it into place, working from top to bottom.

09 Before you remove the film from the window, spray the inside of the glass with the soapy water.

10 Using the tape trick described earlier, separate the protective film from the tint film - as this is done, spray more water onto the outside of the film, to help it separate cleanly. Try not to lift the tint film too much off the glass when separating, as this increases the risk of creasing.

11 Have your helper on standby, to assist with transferring the film to the inside (a prime time for messing it all up). Peel the tint film off the glass, keeping it as flat as you can. Without letting it fold onto itself, move it inside the car and place it accurately on the inside of the glass. The surface which was outside should now be on the inside of the glass (now it's cut it will only fit one way). Carefully slide the film into the corners, keeping it flat (don't crease it) remembering that there must be a tiny gap all round.

13 We found that, to get into the corners (and for tucking the bottom edge of the film into the door), it was easier to unscrew the blade from the squeegee, and use that on its own.

14 Have ready some soft towels - if the excess water is not removed as you go, it will seep back up under the film. Remember, though, you must not squeegee the film when it's dry, so you really end up chasing your tail with this - wetting the film, squeegee-ing, mopping up...

15 Once you've got the film basically in place, it's time to chase out air bubbles and bits which won't stick down - sometimes this is best seen from outside. We found that, after a while, we gave up on the squeegee, and chased some of the bubbles out just using fingers. Don't lift the film off the glass unless absolutely necessary. Remember that persistence pays off - keep at it, and eventually the adhesive will start to dry, and it will stick.

16 Hopefully, you've now got a successfully-tinted window. Don't be tempted to wind the window down for at least two days, and remember that the adhesive can take a week to cure fully. Once it's fully cured, it should be safe to give it a final clean - again, don't use the "banned substances" mentioned earlier and always use a clean soft cloth.

Single wiper

Another saloon-car racing-inspired item, the single wiper conversion is a really smart way to make your Saxo stand out from the crowd. Many Saxo owners want the single wiper because it helps to remove the clutter from the standard Saxo lines - put two Saxos side by side, and the one with one less wiper looks much better. It's a fairly "neutral" mod, too - unlike some, it works well no matter what look you're aiming for.

01 Lift the bonnet, then flip up the covers and undo the wiper nuts. Remove the wiper arms, persuading them off their splines if necessary.

02 Undo the two retaining nuts (one at either end) and one screw (in the middle) and remove the plastic scuttle.

03 Undo the three retaining nuts and remove the wiper motor cover.

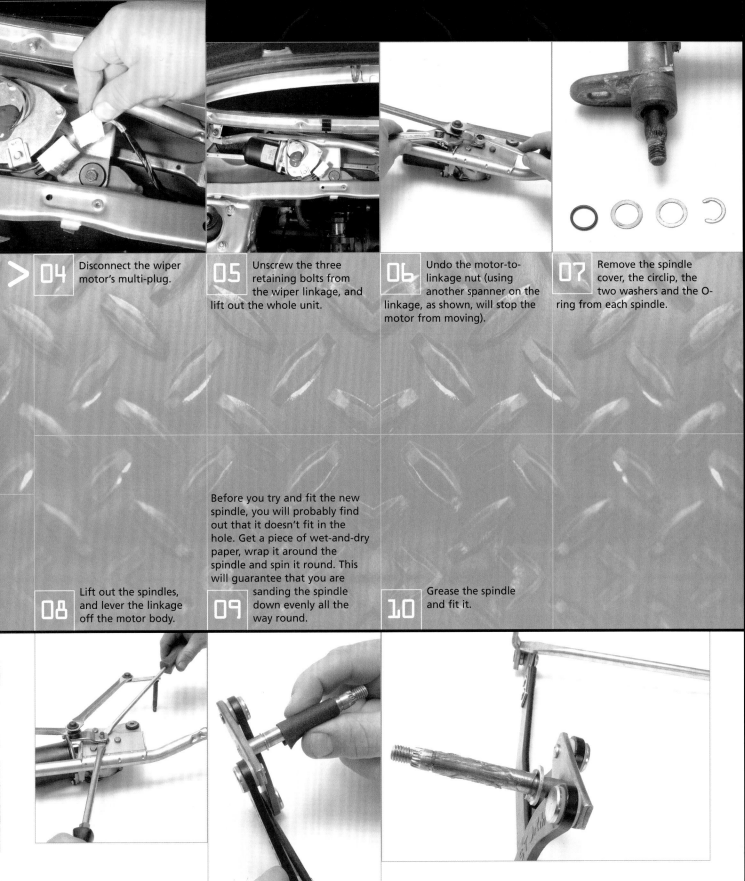

> 04 Disconnect the wiper motor's multi-plug.

05 Unscrew the three retaining bolts from the wiper linkage, and lift out the whole unit.

06 Undo the motor-to-linkage nut (using another spanner on the linkage, as shown, will stop the motor from moving).

07 Remove the spindle cover, the circlip, the two washers and the O-ring from each spindle.

08 Lift out the spindles, and lever the linkage off the motor body.

09 Before you try and fit the new spindle, you will probably find out that it doesn't fit in the hole. Get a piece of wet-and-dry paper, wrap it around the spindle and spin it round. This will guarantee that you are sanding the spindle down evenly all the way round.

10 Grease the spindle and fit it.

11 Refit the O-ring, washers and circlip. You may find that you will have to fit extra washers - you need to fit as many washers as it takes so that the circlip fits correctly, and takes up all the free play on the spindle.

12 Refit the spindle cover.

Refit the motor and linkage back into the car, and reconnect the motor multi-plug. Refit the wiper motor cover and the scuttle. Fit the new wiper arm. If you have not moved the position of the motor, the wiper can be fitted in the rest position (laying flat pointing towards the passenger side). Blank off the hole (with the supplied plug) where the

15 driver's-side wiper used to be.

Now refit the linkage to the motor. Make sure the linkage is fitted like

13 this . . .

. . . and not like this, otherwise the wiper will not wipe the whole screen and will foul the bodywork and make horrible grinding

14 noises.

Painting your Saxo

This is not the section where we tell you how to respray your entire Saxo in a weekend, using only spray cans! This bit's all about how to spray up your various plasticky bits before final fitting - bits such as door mirrors, spoilers, splitters - hell, even bumpers if you like.

As we've no doubt said before, fit your unpainted bits first. Make sure everything fits properly (shape and tidy up all parts as necessary), that all holes have been drilled, and all screws, etc, are doing their job. Then, and only when you're totally, completely happy with the fit - take them off, and get busy with the spray cans.

01 Remove any unwanted "seams" in the plastic, using fine sandpaper or wet-and-dry. Some of these seams look pretty cool, others don't - you decide. With "shiny" plastic, rough-up the surface, or the spray won't "bite" to it. Just take off the shine, no more. You can use fine wet-and-dry for this (used dry), but we like Scotch-Brite, from motor factors and bodyshops.

02 Once the surface has been nicely "roughened", clean up the surface using a suitable degreaser ("suitable" means a type which won't dissolve plastic). Generally, it's ok to use methylated spirit or cellulose thinners (just don't inhale), but test it on a not-so-visible bit first, so you don't have a disaster. The next job is to mask off any areas you don't want painted.

If you like a bit of wildlife in your paint, you can't beat the great outdoors. If it's windy, you'll end up with overspray on everything. Even indoors, if it's damp, you'll have real problems getting a shine - a heater is essential (but not one with a **03** fan - stirring up dust is a no-no). Give the can a good shake. Practice your technique first. Working left-right, then right-left, press the nozzle so you start spraying just before you pass the item, and follow through just past it the other side. Keep the nozzle a constant distance from the item - not in a curved arc. Don't blast the paint on too thick, or you'll have a nasty case of the runs.

Build up thin coats until you've got full coverage, then let it dry for half an hour or more. Using 1000- or 1200-grade wet-and-dry paper (used wet), very lightly sand the whole surface, to take out any minor imperfections. Rinse off **04** thoroughly, then dry the surfaces.

With topcoat, work up from an initial thin mist coat, allowing time for each pass to dry. Any "dry" (dull) patches are usually due to overspray landing on still-wet shiny paint. Don't worry if you can't lose all of these - a light cutting polish will sort it out once the paint's hardened. Blow on a coat or **05** two of clear lacquer - this will also give you your shine.

Tricks 'n' tips

With larger or awkward-shaped items, hang the item up on a piece of string or wire - then you can spin the item round to get the spray into awkward areas.

Ditch your
rear wiper

Rear wipers are undoubtedly useful, and were put there for a good reason, but hey - that's just bor-ing. No smooth tailgate can be seen still wearing a wiper, and in the Saxo's case, you won't even need filler once it's off (mounted through the tailgate glass, innit?). One inexpensive rubber grommet is all you'll need - so get to it!

With the wiper gone, you're free to use the redundant wiper switch to work the tailgate solenoid, as we show you later on...

01 Open the tailgate. Remove the three screws (one at each side, one in the pull handle) securing the trim panel. Release the securing clips and remove the panel.

02 Lift up the wiper nut cover and undo the wiper nut.

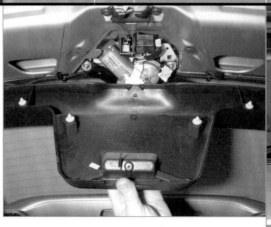

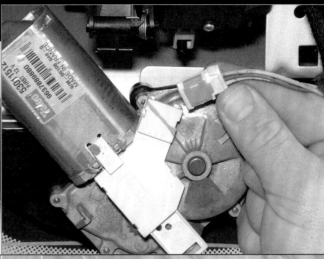

03 Remove the wiper arm from the spindle. We had to use a puller to help us release ours - violence of any other sort is not advisable, or you'll be looking at a busted tailgate glass.

04 When the wiper arm comes free, remove the trim disc underneath, followed by the grommet cover.

05 Disconnect the wiper motor wiring connector . . .

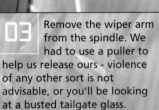

Pull out the washer jet from the top of the car, and detach the jet from the hose. Block up the hose end so that it is water-tight (very important, if you don't want a flooded boot when you use the washers) and drop it back down into the tailgate. Fit a grommet in the washer jet hole to make it water-tight.

06 . . . then undo the three securing nuts and withdraw the motor.

07 Remove the old grommet (with a hole) from the window, and fit a new rubber grommet (without a hole) into the glass, to seal it.

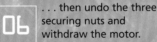
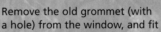
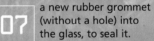
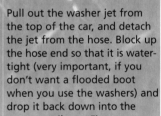

08

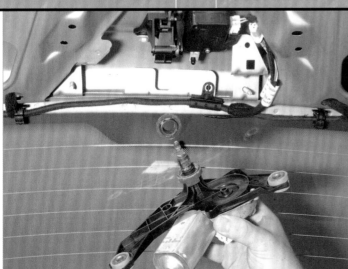

Smoothing the tailgate

Achieving the complete smoothed or "flushed" look isn't too involved a procedure, providing you know someone who can weld, and are handy with the filler and spray. Okay, so it is a bit involved - we cheated and left our Saxo to our local body expert. Very wise.

01 Unscrew and remove the tailgate handle. If you intend to keep the handle on the car and not smooth the back completely, you could always fill the lock hole with filler, and spray it the same colour as the car.

02 Disconnect the tailgate lock multi-plug.

07 Use the template to cut out the same shape from metal plate.

08 Weld the plate into position. While you're at it, you can also weld up the holes for the badges and rear washer jet - well, it's less fiddly than using filler!

09 Using a grinder, smooth down the welded areas.

10 Apply body filler to the welded areas and allow to dry.

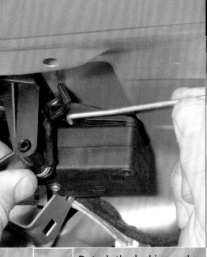

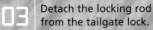

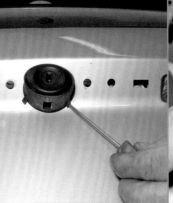

03 Detach the locking rod from the tailgate lock.

04 Unclip the tailgate lock by pushing in the tabs and remove the lock from inside the tailgate. Also remove the number plate lights, making sure you keep the wiring handy - you'll need it for wiring-in your new lights.

05 Using a heat gun, prise off the badges from the rear of the vehicle.

06 Make a card template of the tailgate's number plate recess.

Once dry, sand down the filler to the required shape, but make sure that it is even. You may find that, to achieve the required shape, several applications of filler are required; make sure you sand it down **11** between each application.

Once you have achieved the right shape, apply stopper on top of the filler and allow to dry. Once dry, sand it smooth. Now clean the car thoroughly. Cleaning means not using any polish or silicone, as **12** this will affect the spraying.

13 Once clean, mask up the car. Make sure that all the areas you don't want sprayed are covered up.

Spray the required areas with primer, and allow to dry. Rub down the primer with wet-and-dry paper (wet), then **14** clean all areas and again allow to dry.

Spray the vehicle with the correct body colour. A couple of applications will be required to achieve the desired tone. Allow the paint to dry.
Spray the vehicle again, this time with lacquer, and allow to dry. Once dry, carefully **15** remove the masking, and admire the results.

De-locking

If you're a slave to the smooth Saxo look, by now your door lock barrels will have been annoying you something rotten. If the tailgate's been smoothed and your Saxo's got remote locking, those door locks really are an eyesore - and totally unnecessary. Like the tailgate lock barrel, though, you'll be needing a bit more than a jumbo-sized tin of filler to do the job properly...

01 Remove the door trim panel, using the info in "Interiors". Peel back the door liner, and pull away the lock retaining clip from inside the door.

02 Detach the lock rod from the back of the lock . . .

Unclip the outer door trim panel - this prevents you from melting the plastics when you start welding. You'll also need to shield the plastic door handle somehow, if you haven't removed it like we did.

Make a template of the hole where the door lock was, and create a metal plate of that shape. Weld the door lock plate onto the door, and smooth down the welding with a grinder. Your de-locked door is now ready for spraying.

03 . . . and remove the door lock.

04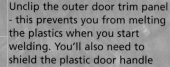

05

Tricks 'n' tips

If the car's battery goes flat, you'll be locked out. We ran a slim wire from each battery terminal, with a 10-amp fuse in the live wire, and the wire ends insulated. The wires were tucked away for access in an emergency, from below. By connecting a slave battery to the wires (don't try jump-starting), you'll get enough juice into the system to work the locks.

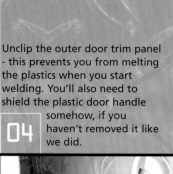

Central locking kit

If your Saxo doesn't have central locking as standard, don't despair - there's several kits out there to help you towards your goal. Our project Saxo already had central locking, so regrettably there are no Saxo-specific photos to show you, but hopefully, the details below, together with your kit's instructions, will help you out.

Before you start fitting your new lock solenoids, it makes sense to test them. Connect them all together as described in your kit's instructions - with power connected to all the solenoids, pull up on the operating plunger of one, and all the rest should pop up too - clever, eh?

Decide where you're going to mount the lock control unit, then identify the various looms, and feed them out to the doors.

The new lock solenoids must be mounted so they work in the same plane as the door lock buttons. What this means is it's no good having the lock solenoid plungers moving horizontally, to work a button and rod which operates vertically. Make up the mounting brackets from the metal bits provided in the kit, and fit the solenoids loosely to the brackets, and to the doors.

The kit contains several items which look like bike spokes - these are your new lock operating rods, which have to be cut to length, then joined onto the old rods using screw clamps. It's best to join the old and new rods at a straight piece of the old rod, so feed the new rod in, and mark it for cutting.

Cut the new rod to the marked length, fit the cut rod to the solenoid, then slip the clamp onto it. Fit the solenoid onto its bracket, and offer the rod into place, to connect to the old rod. Join the new rod and old rod together, and fasten the clamp screws tight. If the clamp screws come loose, you're basically going to be locked out.

Now you can connect up the wires - the easy bit is joining up inside the door. Hopefully, your kit's instructions should be sufficient, but if not, you'll have to resort to the Haynes manual wiring diagrams.

Remote locking

So you can lock and unlock your freshly de-locked doors, you'll need to buy and fit a remote central locking kit, which you can get from several parts suppliers (if you've fitted an alarm, you can get a remote locking interface kit, which will fire the central locking when you zap your alarm keyfob).

To wire up your alarm interface, the best advice is to follow the instructions with the kit - it's impossible to second-guess detailed instructions like this. For what it's worth, though, one piece of advice to bear in mind when tracking down the locking trigger wires is NOT to disconnect the wiring plugs, for testing - the locking system won't work at all if you do, and you won't learn anything.

When you come to test the operation, first make sure at least one window's open, in the unlikely event you lock yourself out. Also check that the doors are locked when the alarm's armed, and not the other way round.

Front arch mods

The law states that no rubber shall protrude from outside your wheelarches, and the MOT crew will not be impressed if your new rubber's rubbing, either. This presents something of a problem, if you're fitting 8-inch wide 17s, especially to a car that's also had a drop job. Even if you've got the right offset alloys (see "Wheels & tyres"), the arches are going to have to be trimmed.

Our wheelarch mods were done at a bodyshop - SAD Motorsport of Yeovil - but if you're brave and reasonably talented, there's nothing to stop you having a go yourself. Best to take the wheels off before you start - have a look in "Wheels & tyres" for info on jacking the car up, if you need to.

01 First to go are the plastic wheelarch liners. Remove the screw securing the wheelarch liner to the bumper.

07 Cut away the plastic lip on the arch trim, to make as much room available as possible for your new wheels. Tidy up the edges using sandpaper.

08 Other tyre-unfriendly wheelarch features can't be overlooked, either. Any sharp edges or protruding objects should be dealt with severely, at the front . . .

09 . . . and at the rear of the wheelarch - remove the bottom lip and flatten any sharp edges.

10 When doing the nearside arch (passenger side), turn the horn round so that it faces forward.

02 Using a suitable forked tool, prise out and remove the push-in securing clips. Ensure that nothing else in the wheelarch is preventing removal, then manipulate the liner out.

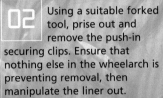

03 Remove the bumper as described later in "Bodykits". Unclip and remove the side repeater.

04 Unscrew the one retaining screw and unclip the wheelarch trim. The push-in clips are like the ones used to hold your outer door trims on.

05 Mark up the arch for trimming, just below the trim clip holes. Don't cut above the clip holes, or you'll struggle to get the wheelarch trim back on.

06 Cut off the bit of arch you don't need, and debur any rough edges. Paint the newly-cut edges to prevent any rust from forming. It's also wise to apply some wax treatment for added protection.

. . . and after shots - spot the difference? The top corner lug and lower tongue had to go. This is the standard bumper - obviously, a bodykit might require different surgery. Replace the wheelarch trim and refit the bumper. When fitting the bumper, you'll have to drill a new hole so that you can screw the bumper and the plastic trim together.

On the driver's side, you'll have to elongate the washer bottle mounting hole so that the washer bottle can be moved forward (area to cut off is highlighted in the picture). The minimum amount that the bottle should be moved is half an inch, to give clearance on full lock. Also prevents you rubbing a hole in your washer bottle. The front arches should now be completely sorted.

11 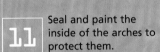 Seal and paint the inside of the arches to protect them.

12 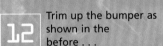 Trim up the bumper as shown in the before . . .

13 screw the bumper and the plastic trim together.

14 should now be completely sorted.

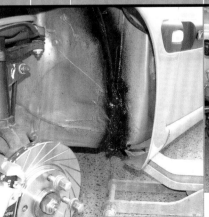

Rear arch mods

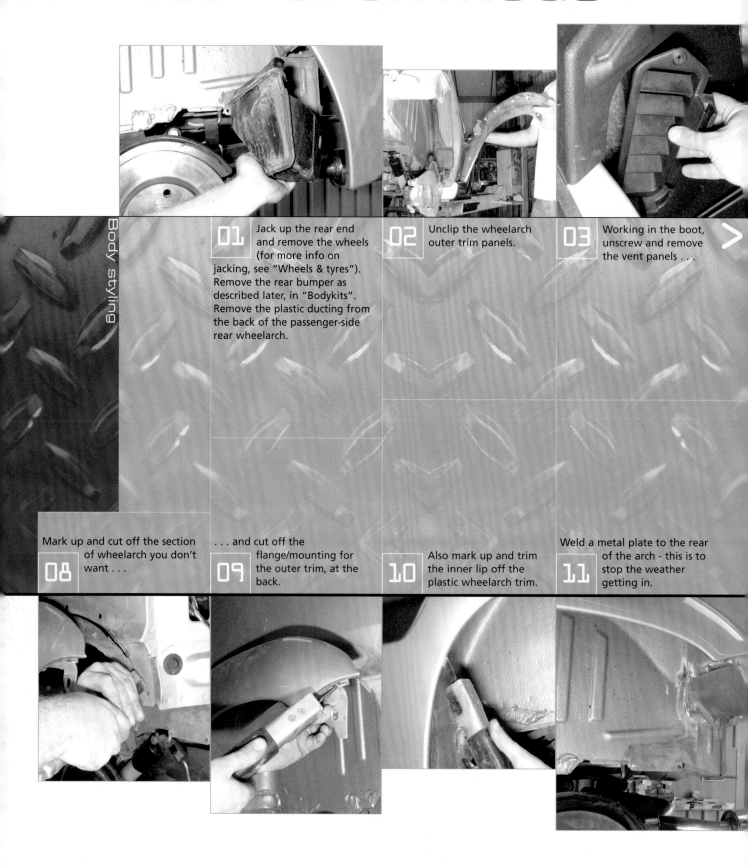

01 Jack up the rear end and remove the wheels (for more info on jacking, see "Wheels & tyres"). Remove the rear bumper as described later, in "Bodykits". Remove the plastic ducting from the back of the passenger-side rear wheelarch.

02 Unclip the wheelarch outer trim panels.

03 Working in the boot, unscrew and remove the vent panels . . .

08 Mark up and cut off the section of wheelarch you don't want . . .

09 . . . and cut off the flange/mounting for the outer trim, at the back.

10 Also mark up and trim the inner lip off the plastic wheelarch trim.

11 Weld a metal plate to the rear of the arch - this is to stop the weather getting in.

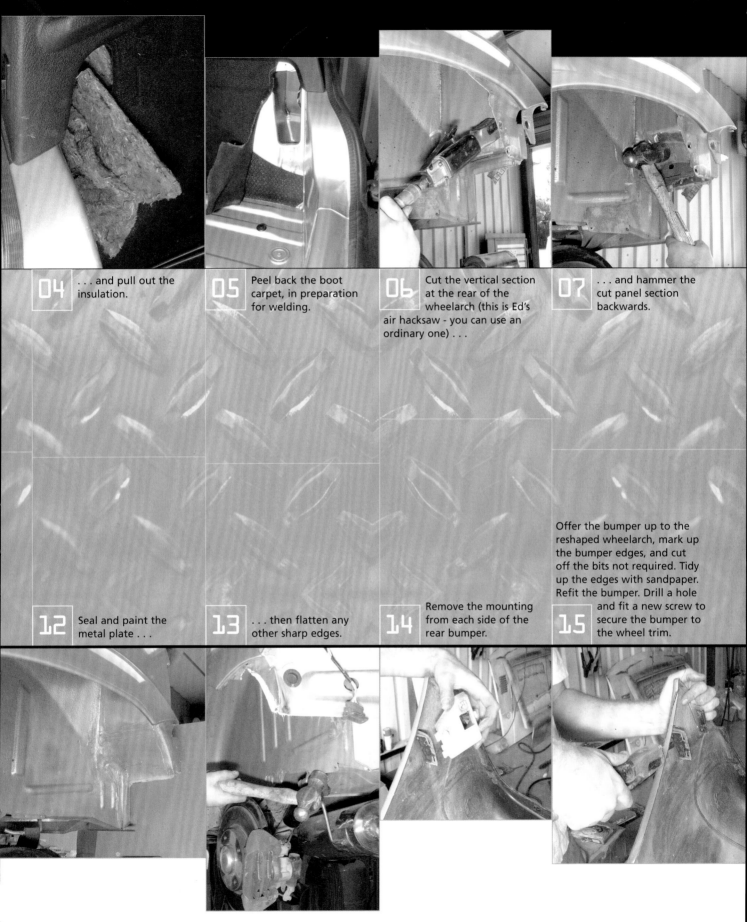

04 . . . and pull out the insulation.

05 Peel back the boot carpet, in preparation for welding.

06 Cut the vertical section at the rear of the wheelarch (this is Ed's air hacksaw - you can use an ordinary one) . . .

07 . . . and hammer the cut panel section backwards.

12 Seal and paint the metal plate . . .

13 . . . then flatten any other sharp edges.

14 Remove the mounting from each side of the rear bumper.

15 Offer the bumper up to the reshaped wheelarch, mark up the bumper edges, and cut off the bits not required. Tidy up the edges with sandpaper. Refit the bumper. Drill a hole and fit a new screw to secure the bumper to the wheel trim.

Bodykits

Bodykits are straightforward to fit, and look cool. Thanks to the popularity of the Jap look, Wings West from California have come to the forefront of the market, with their evil-looking creations.

A number of other companies produce similar kits, and the theory is largely the same for fitting all types - it's a mixture of bonding and screwing on spoilers and skirts. Always trial-fit before you spray - we had to make adjustments to the kit to get it to fit, so left ours black until we were happy.

It's worth checking out what material is used - for example, fibreglass isn't very flexible, and could crack easily. When it comes to spraying, you'll need to know what type of primer to use. Don't forget weight - if you're adding a ton of filler and plastic to your car, you're going to need a bigger engine to drag it all round.

One last thing - find somebody who's fitted the kit you want, or who has bought from the same company. Was the finish any good? Did it fit okay? You might save yourself a lot of trouble...

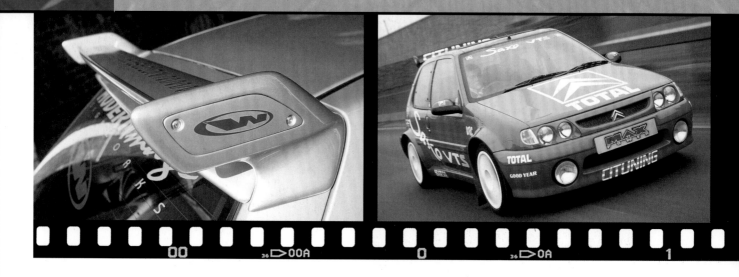

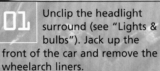 Unclip the headlight surround (see "Lights & bulbs"). Jack up the front of the car and remove the wheelarch liners.

Remove the screw on each side securing the bumper end to the bodywork.

Front bumper removal

Unscrew the two securing screws from the bottom edge of the bumper. Disconnect the front foglight wiring, and the washer tubes from the headlight washers. Unclip the bumper end at each side, then pull the bumper forwards to disengage the two locating clips from the front panel, and remove it from the front of the car.

Working under each wheelarch, unscrew the bumper securing bolt at the side and the one at the front.

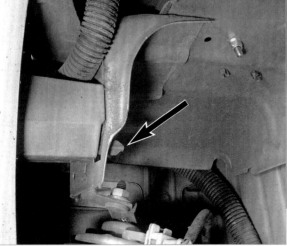

Rear bumper removal

01 Open the tailgate, then unscrew and remove the rear tail lights.

02 Jack up the rear of the car, then unclip and remove the rear wheelarch liners.

03 Remove the two bolts securing the plastic outer part of the bumper to the inner (metal) bumper bar.

04 Remove the two bolts (one each side), which secure the bumper to the bodywork.

05 Remove the two plastic screws from the bumper and remove the plastic bumper.

06 Unbolt and remove the metal bumper bar from the car.

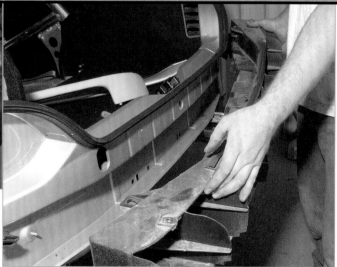

Bodykit fitting

First thing to do is work out what's what, make sure you know where everything goes and how it fits. Also make sure that everything you want is there, even so far as making sure the kit is the right one for your car... These are the front and rear lower bumpers for a Saxo.
 01

Trial fitting stuff is important, here we are offering up the rear lower bumper. You're checking here for things like towing eyes lining up, if you've fitted twin exhausts, you may have to cut out a section for these or anything else you've added. Also check any mounting points.
 02

While you're trial fitting the kit, mark where the bumper sits and make sure it's level from side to side, holding it on, use a pen and tape measure to check this. Get this bit wrong, and the world will not be your oyster...
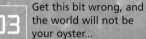 03

The rear lower bumper wraps around the original Citroën part and screws into the rear edge of the wheelarch - trouble is we've cut this off to enable us to fit 17s. This is a problem you're likely to have if you've fitted large rims. However, anything is possible...
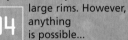 04

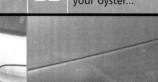

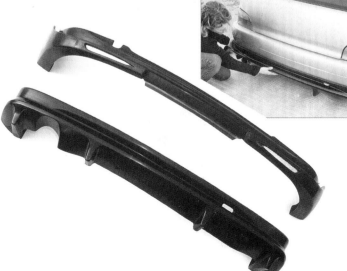

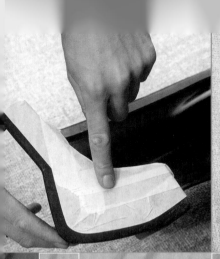

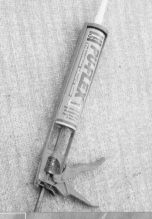

05 We're going to bond it on instead of screwing it, as obviously there's nothing to screw to. Because of this, we can cut off the excess to allow us to keep our 17s. Mark up the unwanted material with masking tape, then use a jigsaw or hacksaw to cut it off.

06 We're going to use a polyurethane adhesive, which pretty much does what it says on the tube. There are a lot of different types of adhesive available, so make sure you get the right one for the materials you're using.

07 Make sure the area you're applying it to is clean and free from dirt, it's also worth scoring it with a nail or other sharp object, to give the adhesive something to grip into, like when you sand bodywork before painting it. Also make sure the kit sits flush on the bodywork at this point.

08 Instead of adhesives, the Wings West kit uses a double-sided tape on the leading edge, so after you've worked out the correct fitting level you've got to clean this line as well. Wings West supply a specially formulated cleaner, but a decent panel wipe will suffice.

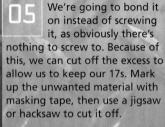

Where we've modfied our lower grille by fitting mesh, the kit cannot enter as it's designed to. You may come across problems like this - if so, see if the part is structural. Ours isn't, so we can cut it off - or cut slots in the mesh to slip the bumper through. **13**

We elected to cut it off. It might seem strange having to modify something that's supposed to be modified already, but manufacturers can't take into account every possible modification you've thought of. So use your swede and do it yourself. Just make sure if you start cutting, you know what you're doing. **14**

As with the rear bumper, we're going to bang the front on after we've had to cut off the excess on the inner arch. Always remember to clean and score the surface and make sure it actually touches the kit to ensure it's not going to pull off. **15**

Now it's time for the rear spoiler. Offer it up (surprise, surprise). Measure and make sure it's level, then mark up its position. This is a little more complicated, as it involves drilling the bodywork. **16**

09 When you're ready to fit your kit, pull a couple of inches of backing from the tape at each end. Pull the backing up at ninety degrees and offer up the bumper.

10 Obviously we haven't sprayed our kit yet, but at this stage in the fitting, you pull the backing from the tape and secure the kit as you go along. Eventually you'll meet the other end in the middle somewhere, and your bumper will be secured.

11 Now we've moved on to the side skirts. We've removed the front and rear wheels so that we can get at the inner arches. As with the rear bumper section, you have to secure the side skirt to the inner arch. You have to drill holes in the arch for this - make sure the holes are rust-proofed and painted before final fitting takes place.

12 The front bumper is now offered up. Now we've got a problem - the front wheels on full lock foul on the trailing edges. It's always worth doing a job like trial fitting with two people - whilst one person holds, another can mark or measure.

Remove the mounting screws, and pay attention to the warning - it's true. Due to manufacturing processes, it could blow apart, highly amusing - but dangerous and expensive. Make sure that holes like these aren't blocked when sprayed. **17**

Wings West use a clever marker technique to find where you need to drill the bodywork. You insert these black plastic strips in the spoiler mount holes, and hold the spoiler up to the bodywork. Tape them on to the bodywork and remove the spoiler. **18**

You now have a perfect marker for the mount hole. When you drill through a panel, always make sure you've checked the other side for cables, sound proofing and trim panels. As before, when drilled, rust proof the holes and use a touch up pen to paint them. **19**

If you're feeling confident, you can have a go at spraying the kit yourself, although we wouldn't recommend it. This is what the finished kit looks like on a Saxo, tough and distinctive. It's not just a case of bolting it on, but with a days work and bit of patience, you can do it at home. **20**

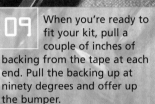

CAUTION!!! DO NOT BLOW AIR INTO, OR FILL THIS HOLE, SPOILER WILL EXPLODE

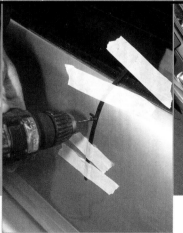

Rear diffuser

Rear diffusers look best on cars which have been seriously dropped, and if care is taken on your choice of exhaust system (or just the rear box), the combination of diffuser and rear pipes can really "tone up" that rear end! A twin-exit exhaust like ours, for instance, is just crying out for a diffuser, and we didn't want to disappoint.

01 Mark up the rear bumper so you know where to drill the two mounting holes (two on each side that is) for the diffuser. Drill the holes.

02 Screw the diffuser in place. Simple as that. Maybe we should've suggested to Ed that this would be easier with the car jacked up - but he obviously likes a challenge.

03 Now check the details - if you're not happy with the fit, the diffuser can come off again, and get treated with the sander. It pays to get the profile just right - looks a lot less "bolt-on", if you make an effort at this stage.

04 Now that you know it fits, you can get it sprayed. You can either spray it yourself or get someone else to do it, like we did. Over to you, Ed...

Bonnet **vents**

Once you've got your bodykit on, you may well want to fit some kind of bonnet vent. This is a very tricky job to tackle yourself, unless you're really that good, or that brave. Leave it in the hands of the professionals is our advice. Plenty of options - you can get little louvres stamped in as well, to complement your Evo, Impreza, Integrale or Celica GT4 vent. Or you could go for something more original. There are even people using the bonnet scoop from a Kia Sedona people carrier! Truly, anything goes.

Lights & bulbs

Apart from important things like style and general coolness, check whether your fave lights are UK-legal (they should have an E-marking and be suitable for right-hand drive). If they're not, expect trouble at MOT time. Popular headlight mods include fitting uprated headlight bulbs and/or colour-coded eyebrows. Or you could junk the original lights completely, in favour of a neat quad headlight conversion.

Headlight bulbs

The high-power and "blue" headlight bulbs boost headlight performance, and give more of a unique look. However, fitting bulbs is not without its pitfalls. Some bulbs are illegal for use in this country, being too powerful, so ask before you buy.

Even if you're not bothered about the legality of high-power bulbs, be aware that any increase in power will also result in an increase in the heat they produce (and we're talking about bulbs well over 60W/55 here). Excessive bulb heat could damage the headlight reflectors/lenses, and the excess current draw could damage wiring.

01 Nice and simple one, this. The procedure is shown on a "Phase II" model, but is equally applicable to a "Phase I" Saxo. Open the bonnet and disconnect the main wiring plug from the rear of the headlight unit.

Tricks 'n' tips
When handling the bulbs, do not touch the glass. This will decrease the life of the bulb dramatically. If it is accidentally touched, wipe it clean using methylated spirit.

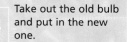

02 Peel off the rubber cover from the rear of the headlight, noting how it fits over the bulb terminals.

03 Press together the looped ends of the bulb retaining clip and release it from the rear of the light unit.

04 Take out the old bulb and put in the new one.

Headlight **eyebrows**

01 First, take your headlight eyebrows and spray them the required colour (for info on spraying, refer to "Body styling"). Fix the Velcro strips to the rear of the eyebrow, along the bottom edge. Obviously, the velcro shouldn't protrude below the brow.

Clean the headlight thoroughly - getting ALL the dead bugs off, which could take a while. **02**

Offer the eyebrow into position, then carefully remove the backing from the Velcro and stick into place. **03**

Twin headlight
conversion ("Phase II")

A more expensive option is to go for twin headlights, available as a kit from the French company Morette. These aren't cheap, but they look truly superb once the light surrounds have been sprayed. Fitting is relatively straightforward, and the finished result is majorly worth it.

01 First, if you've got headlight adjusters, make sure they're set to the normal position, or position '0'. Open up the bonnet and disconnect the battery negative lead.

Remove the screw securing the headlight lower trim panel in position. Carefully free the trim panel clip situated underneath the headlight unit and remove the panel. Be warned; the clip is fragile and is easily broken if not released carefully. **02**

Unscrew the three retaining bolts and move the light unit forward. **03**

Disconnect the wiring connectors from the headlight and sidelight bulbs and (where fitted) from the headlight levelling motor (note which one does what, for later), and remove the headlight. **04**

>

05 Repeat Steps 2 to 4 and remove the other headlight.

06 Where fitted, remove the headlight alignment motor from the original headlight (bayonet fitment, twist and pull), and fit it to the new headlights.

07 Make sure that the ball-ended fitment locates into the adjustment arm, as shown in the picture.

>

11 Connect all the wiring multi-plugs to the back of the lights . . .

12 . . . then bolt the headlight into place using the three bolts.

08 Locate the earthing wire for the new headlights, and attach it to an earthing point.

09 Remove the headlight surround from the new lights by removing the four screws.

10 Fit a speed clip to the front wing - this will be used to secure the new headlight in place.

Don't forget to set the headlight aim. Accurate adjustment will mean a garage with beam-setting equipment, but this isn't an expensive job, and it's worth it to get the best from your new lights. A rough setting can be made using a garage door or a wall - use the light maker's info for the location of the adjusters.

13 Run the power wire up to the fusebox and secure as shown.

14 Secure the headlight fuse into the fusebox - it's a good idea to label it for easy identification.

15 Refit the headlight surround, and check for a decent fit. If no trimming is needed, you can remove the headlight surrounds again and colour-code them.

16 [continues from the paragraph above]

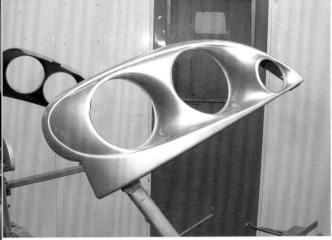

Twin headlight
conversion ("Phase I")

Okay, okay - not everyone's got a "Phase II" Saxo like ours. The following section is a potted version of how to fit a conversion kit to Saxo "Phase I" models (are we good to you, or what?).

Open up the bonnet and disconnect the battery negative lead. Use a long screwdriver between the right-hand headlight unit and indicator to depress the retaining clip, then slide the indicator out of position and disconnect the wiring connector. Repeat the procedure and remove the left-hand indicator.

Carefully prise off the U-shaped retaining clip from each end of the radiator grille panel, then remove the three bolts securing the top of the grille panel to the body. Carefully free the grille panel ends from the wings, then slide the panel forwards to release its clips and free it from the car. The panel is retained by two clips situated underneath each headlight unit. Be warned; these clips are fragile and are easily broken if not released carefully.

Disconnect the wiring connectors from the right-hand headlight and sidelight bulbs and (where fitted) from the headlight levelling motor - note which one does what, for later.

Unscrew the retaining bolt from the top and bottom of the right-hand headlight. Carefully unclip the top of the light unit from the crossmember, then slide the light unit forwards to release it from its L-shaped lower locating lugs. Remove the light unit. Disconnect the wiring and fasteners the same way, and remove the left-hand headlight.

Installation of the kit should be straightforward (most kits use the same mounting points as the standard Citroën components). Follow the instructions supplied with the kit, and check the operation of the headlights and indicators before using the car on the road. Set the headlight aim using the info previously given for the "Phase II" kit.

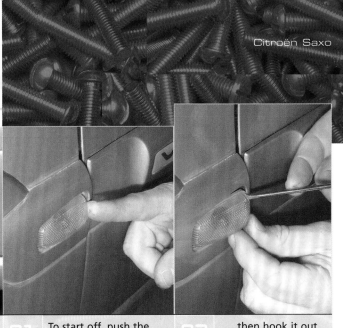

Side
repeaters

Although the side repeaters on the VTR/S are cooler than most standard items (they're usually clear), that's no reason to leave them standard. How about whipping them out for a light blast of light-tinting spray, to colour-match them to the car? Then there's all the other wacky colours, smoked ones, crystal ones - suddenly, standard doesn't look so hot.

01 To start off, push the repeater light forwards . . .

02 . . . then hook it out at the back end.

03 Now you can either take the light out completely, and disconnect the black wiring plug (take care that the plug doesn't disappear into the wing, though) . . .

04 . . . or, if you've got new lenses which fit the old bulb holders, just twist and pull off the old lens, and smack on the new one - simple.

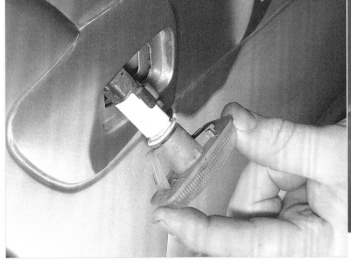

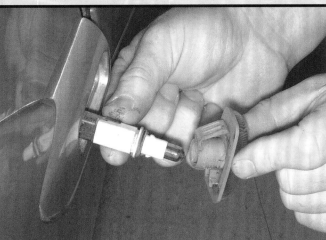

Rear lights

Available in as many colours as the side repeaters, coloured rear light clusters are very popular among the modded Saxo fraternity. You can opt for smoked, clear, coloured, Lexus style, or quad rear lights. We opted for colour-coding the lights using a thin coat of body-coloured paint/laquer.

When buying rear light clusters, once again, it's not a good idea to go for the cheapest you can find, because you'll be buying trouble. Cheap rear light clusters are usually for left-hand-drive only (typically, they're made for the Euro market, and will only carry TUV approval). The problem concerns rear foglights and rear reflectors, both of which your rear lights must have, to be legal. Getting around this problem, if your lights aren't legal straight out of the box, is too much grief - so buy UK-legal lights.

01 Removing the old lights is quite remarkably easy - no tools required, even. Open the tailgate, and undo the large black plastic nut. From this point on, the light could fall out at any time, so be ready.

02 Pull the light unit out, taking care not to strain the wiring to the bulbholder.

03 Two options now, for light removal - either release the tab at the outer edge of the light unit, and take out the bulbholder . . .

04 . . . or (preferably) use a thin screwdriver to release the spring clip securing the bulbholder wiring plug, and take off the complete light unit.

Light
tinting

We handed our lights over to Ed Short at SAD Motorsport in Yeovil, who sprayed them to match the body colour of the car. The spray was made up of the manufacturer's paint colour, mixed with a lot of lacquer, to make it nearly-transparent.

01 Once the lights are out, give them a good clean - any silicone polish that's been used on the car will prevent the paint from sticking. Meths is a pretty safe bet for cleaning purposes, but give the lights a good wipe with a clean, dry rag or towel even after this.

The trick with light-tinting by spraying is to put the paint on evenly. You'll need more than the suggested two coats to get a decent effect, but you will see the effect of one light coat on any previously-clear lens. Obviously, it helps if both rear lights get the same number of coats… Don't go too dark with any colour though, if you don't want to get pulled every 5 minutes.

A quick bit of masking-up later, and you're ready to get spraying.
02

03

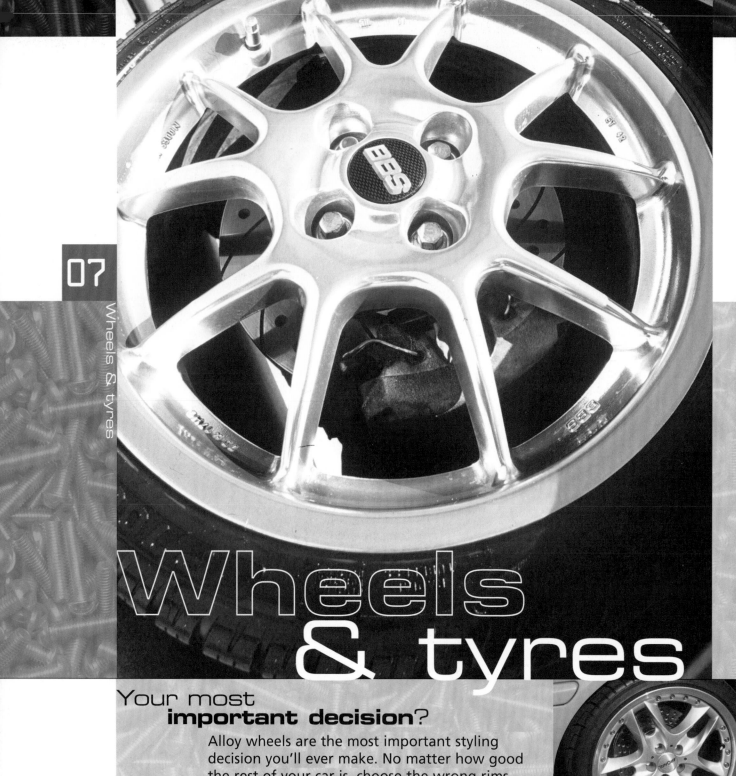

Wheels & tyres

Your most important decision?

Alloy wheels are the most important styling decision you'll ever make. No matter how good the rest of your car is, choose the wrong rims and your car will never look right. Choose a good set and you're already well on the way to creating a sorted motor. Take your time and pick wisely - wheel fashions change like the weather, and you don't want to spend shedloads on a set of uncool alloys.

1

Alloys and insurance

Before we go any further into which wheels are right for you, a word about insurance and security. Fitting tasty alloys to your Saxo is one of the first and best ways to make it look cool. It follows, therefore, that someone of low moral standing might very well want to unbolt them from your car while you're not around.

Since fitting a set of alloys is one of the easiest bolt-on ways to mod a car, it's no surprise that the market in stolen alloys is as alive and kicking as it currently is. It's also not unknown for a set of wheels to go missing just for the tyres - if you've just splashed out on a set of fat Yokohamas, your wheels look even more tempting.

Tell your insurance company what you're fitting. They'll ask for the details, but are unlikely to charge you extra. You'll have to accept that they won't cover the extra cost of the wheels if they get nicked (or if the whole car goes). If you want the rims covered, it's best to talk to a company specialising in modified cars, or you could be asked to pay out the wheel cost again in premiums. The dumbest thing you can do is say nothing, and hope they don't find out - we don't want to go on about this, but there are plenty of documented cases where insurance companies have refused to pay out altogether, purely on the basis of undeclared alloy wheels.

Cheap alloys?

Hopefully, you'll be deciding which wheels to go for based on how they look, not how much they cost, but inevitably (for most ordinary people at least), price does become a factor. Some of the smaller manufacturers recognise this, and offer cheaper copies of more expensive designs - this is fine as far as you're concerned, but what's the catch? Surely buying a cheaper wheel must have its pitfalls? Well, possibly - and some of them may not be so obvious.

Inevitably, cheaper wheels equal lower quality and may be made from lesser-grade alloys, and may not be subjected to the same exacting tests as those from the top manufacturers. The worst case scenario is that you could end up with a wheel which is slightly "porous".

The main disadvantage of porosity in an alloy wheel is that the air will leak slowly out, and over a matter of time the tyre will deflate. We're not saying the tyre will deflate overnight, but porosity could result in a loss of for example say 5 psi a week. If you check your tyre pressures every week, this will be no more than a bit of an inconvenience. A tyre running 5 psi down will effect the handling of the car and also result in the tyre scrubbing out quickly. If you don't check the pressures for two weeks, then the tyre is 10 psi down, and now we're talking dodgy handing and nasty tyre wear, not to mention the possibility of a tyre blow-out.

Porous wheels also have difficulty in retaining their paint or lacquer finish, with flaking a known problem. If the lacquer or paint comes off, the alloy is then exposed to the elements. Keeping your alloys clean can be a chore at the best of times, but once the lacquer or paint starts to deteriorate, the brake dust and dirt will become ingrained in the surface of the alloy. Serious effort every time you clean, and the problem will only get worse - the more you scrub, the more the lacquer comes off. Add to this the joys of the British winter (salt + exposed alloy = corrosion) and your wheels will start to look very second-hand, very quickly.

Buying wheels from established, popular manufacturers with a large range has another hidden benefit, too. It stands to reason that choosing a popular wheel will mean that more suppliers will stock it, and the manufacturers themselves will make plenty of them. Okay, so what? Well, if you're unlucky enough to have an accident which results in non-repairable damage to one wheel, you're going to need a replacement. If you've chosen the rarest wheels on the planet, you could be faced with having to replace a complete set of four, to get them all matching… A popular wheel, even if it's a few years old, might be easier to source.

Keep them clean

It's a small point maybe, but you'll obviously want your wheels to look as smart as possible, as often as possible - so how easy are they going to be to clean? The multi-spokers are hell to clean - a toothbrush job - do you really want this much aggro every week? The simpler the design, the easier time you'll have. There are plenty of good products out there to make your life less of a cleaning nightmare, but stay away from the very strong cleaners which can do more harm than good.

Locking bolts

Don't forget about locking wheel bolts (see "Hold on to your wheels" further on) - bargain these into a wheel/tyre package if you're buying new.

Other options

If you're on a really tight budget, and perhaps own a base model Saxo, don't overlook the possibility of fitting a set of standard alloys discarded by a VTR/VTS owner - check that the bolt pattern's the same, obviously (a lot of early Saxos have three bolts per wheel, later models have four).

Tricks 'n' tips
If you're keeping a steel wheel as your spare (or even if you're keeping an original alloy), keep a set of your original wheel bolts in a bag inside the spare wheel. Locking bolts especially might be too long when fitted to a thin steel wheel, and might jam up your brakes.

Tricks 'n' tips
It's worth applying a bit of car polish to the wheels - provided it's good stuff, and you can be sure of getting the residue out of the corners and edges, a polished wheel will always be easier to clean off than an unpolished one.

Size matters

The trend in wheel size is an interesting one. It seems that, for us Brits, biggest is best - there are Saxos out there with 18s and up. But in general it's safe to say that you can't be seen with anything less than 17-inchers. In Europe, meanwhile, they're mad for the small-wheel look, still with seriously dropped suspension of course, but on 14- and 15-inch rims. On many cars (the Saxo included), 16-inch rims are the biggest you can sensibly fit before you really have to start looking at sorting the arches. In fact, on the Saxo, we wouldn't rule out the possibility of some arch massaging, even on 16s, especially if you're determined to slam the car down.

Successfully fitting big wheels in combination with lowered suspension is one of the major challenges to the modifier. With the Saxo being a modern, small hatchback there's not as much space under the arches as on some other vehicles. As much as anything, it's tyre width that ultimately leads to problems, not so much the increased wheel diameter.

If the tyres are simply too wide, they will first of all rub on the suspension strut (ie on the inside edge of the tyre). Also, the inside edges may rub on the arches on full steering lock - check left and right. Rubbing on the inside edges can be cured by fitting spacers or offsets between the wheel and hub, which effectively move the wheel outwards, "spacing" it away from its normal position (this also has the effect of widening the car's track, which may improve the on-limit handling - or not). Fitting spacers must be done using special longer wheel bolts, as the standard ones may only engage into the hubs by a few threads, which is highly dangerous (also check that your locking bolts are long enough).

Rubbing on the outside edges is a simple case of wheelarch lip fouling, which must be cured by rolling out and cutting off the wheelarch return edge, and other mods. If you've gone for really wide tyres, the outer edge of the tyre will probably be visible outside the wheelarch, and this is a no-no (it's illegal, and you must cover it up). The only solution there is to fit a wide-arch kit.

The other trick with fitting immense alloys is of course to avoid the "4x4 off-roader" look, which you will achieve remarkably easily just by bolting on a set of 17s with standard suspension. The massive increase in ground clearance is fine for a bit of off-roading, but won't win much admiration at a cruise. Overcoming this problem can be a matter almost of inspired guesswork, as much as anything - especially if the budget won't stretch to a set of coilovers (see "Suspension").

Jargon explained

PCD – Is your Pitch Circle Diameter, which relates to the spacing of your wheel bolt holes, or "stud pattern". It is expressed by the diameter of a notional circle which passes through the centre of your wheel bolts, and the number of bolts. If, for instance, the PCD is 100 mm with four bolts, it's given as 100/4.

ROLLING RADIUS – is the distance from the wheel centre to the outer edge of the tyre, or effectively, half the overall diameter.

OFFSET - this is determined by the distance from the wheel mounting face in relation to its centre-line. The offset figure is denoted by ET (no, I mustn't), which stands for einpress tiefe in German, or pressed-in depth (now I know you're asleep). The lower the offset, the more the wheels will stick out. Fitting wheels with the wrong offset might bring the wheel into too-close contact with the brake and suspension bits, or with the arches. Very specialised area - seek advice from the wheel manufacturers if you're going for a very radical size (or even if you're not).

Speedo error?

One side-effect of fitting massive wheels is that your car appears to go slower. As the wheel diameter increases, so does its circumference (distance around the outside) - this means that, to travel say one mile, a large wheel will turn less than a smaller wheel. Therefore, for a given actual speed, since the method for measuring speed is the rate of wheel rotation, a car with larger wheels will produce a lower speedo reading than one with smaller wheels - but it's not actually going any slower in reality. With the ever-increasing number of speed cameras around, even doing an indicated 35 in a 30 limit becomes really dodgy on big wheels - you could in fact be doing 40, and that's pointsville. This is not a great problem, just remember to compensate accordingly when driving in 30 and 40 zones.

The effects of increased wheel size are masked slightly by the fact that, as wheel size goes up, tyre profile (sidewall height) comes down, so one or two inches on wheel diameter might not mean any increase in overall wheel and tyre diameter.

Obviously, you must carry the special key or tool which came with your bolts with you at all times, in case of a puncture, or if you're having any other work done, such as new brakes or tyres. The best thing to do is rig this onto your keyring, so that it's with you, but not left in the car. Don't leave it in the glovebox or the boot...that's the first place they'll look.

Hold on to your wheels

The trouble with fitting big wheels is that they are bolted on, and are just as easily bolted off, if you don't make life difficult for the thieves. If you have to park outside at night, you could wake up one morning to a car that's literally been slammed on the deck. Add to this the fact that your car isn't going anywhere without wheels, plus the damage which will be done to exhaust, fuel and brake pipes from dropping on its belly, and it's suddenly a lot worse than losing a grand's worth of wheels and tyres.

The market and demand for stolen alloys is huge, and most people don't bother having them security-marked in any way, so once a set of wheels disappears, they're almost impossible to trace. Security marking won't prevent the wheels from being stolen but it does have a deterrent effect It.

When choosing that car alarm, try and get one with an "anti-jacking" feature, because the thieves hate it. Imagine a metal saucer, with a metal ball sitting on a small magnet in the centre. If the saucer tilts in any direction, the ball rolls off the magnet, and sets off the alarm. Highly sensitive, and death to anyone trying to lift your car up for the purpose of removing the wheels. Simply having an alarm with anti-shock is probably not good enough, because a careful villain will probably be able to work so as not to create a strong enough vibration to trigger it.

Cheap locking wheel bolts will be effective as a deterrent to the inexpert thief (kids, in other words), but will probably only slow down the pro. If you fit a cheap set of locking bolts, they will use a hammer and thin chisel to crack off the locking bolt heads. Some bolts can easily be defeated by hammering a socket onto the bolt head, and undoing the locking bolt as normal, while some of the key-operated bolts are so pathetic that they can be beaten using a small screwdriver. So it's vital to choose the best bolts you can.

There seems to be some debate as to whether it's okay to fit more than one set of locking bolts to a car - some people value their wheels so highly that they've fitted three or four sets of bolts. The feeling against doing this is that the replacement locking bolts may not be made to the same standard as factory originals, and while it's okay to fit one set on security grounds, fitting more than that is dangerous on safety grounds should the locking bolts not be up to the required standard.

Tricks 'n' tips

A word of warning about re-using your existing wheel bolts, should you be upgrading from steel wheels. Most steel-wheel bolts are not suitable for use with alloy wheels (and vice-versa). Make sure you ask about this when buying new wheels, and if necessary, bargain a set of bolts into the price.

Another point to watch for is that the new wheel bolts are the correct length for your fitment, taking into account whether you've fitted spacers or not. Bolts that are too short are obviously dangerous, and ones that are too long can foul on drum brakes, and generally get in the way of any turning activities. If in doubt ask the retailer for advice. Always check that the wheels turn freely once they've been put on, and investigate any strange noises before you go off for a pose.

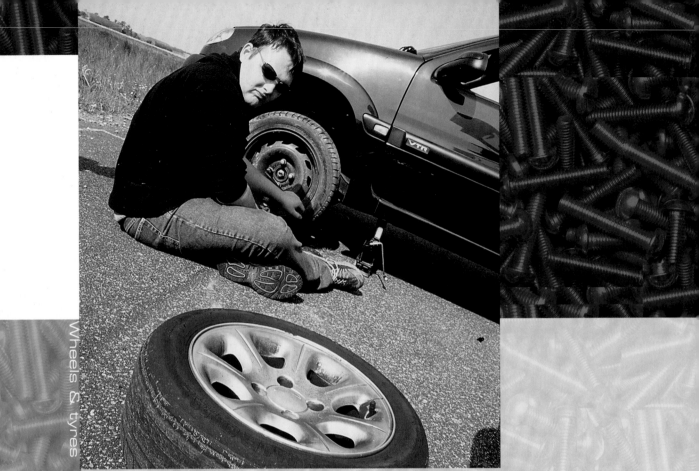

Changing a set of wheels

You might think you know all about this, but do you really? Okay, so you know you need a jack and wheelbrace (or socket and ratchet), but where are the jacking points? If you want to take more than one wheel off at a time, have you got any axle stands, and where do they go? If you've only ever had wheels and tyres fitted by a garage, chances are you're actually a beginner at this. It's surprising just how much damage you can do to your car, and to yourself, if you don't know what you're doing.

What to use

If you don't already have one, invest in a decent hydraulic (trolley) jack and a set of axle stands. The standard Citroën jack supplied with the vehicle just isn't stable enough to rely on for anything else other than an emergency wheel change.

Lifting and lowering the car is so much easier with a trolley jack, and once the axle stands are in position, there's no way the car can come down on you. Never rely purely on the jack for support - remember that even a brand-new trolley jack could creep down if you haven't tightened the release valve fully, or possibly fail completely under load. In the same way, never be tempted to use bricks, wooden blocks or anything else which you have to pile up, to support the car.

When using a hydraulic jack or axle stand, it's good practice to place a block of wood between the jack/stand head and car. This helps to spread the load over a wider area, avoiding damage to the underside of the car, and also protecting the underbody coating. Cut a slot in the top of the block of wood; this slot can then be engaged with the lower lip of the sill when positioning the jack/stand under the sill jacking points.

Trolley jack under one of the front support points, and an axle stand under the sill jacking point.

Where to use it

If possible, always jack the car up on a solid, level surface (ideally, a concrete or tarmac driveway). Jacking up on a rough or gravelled surface is not recommended, as the car's weight won't be evenly distributed, and the jack may slip. If you have to jack up the vehicle on a surface which isn't level, be sure to firmly chock at least one of the other wheels so that the car doesn't roll away as it is lifted. It's good practice to chock a wheel, even if the ground is 100% level.

Jacking up the front

Before jacking up the front of the car, pull the handbrake on firmly (you can also chock the rear wheels, if you don't trust your handbrake).

If you're taking the wheels off, loosen the wheel bolts before you start jacking up the car. It's easily forgotten, but you'll look pretty silly trying to undo the wheel bolts with the front wheels spinning in mid-air. Standard alloys might have an anti-theft cover fitted over the bolts, or one locking bolt - you'll need the special key (probably in the glovebox!).

We'll assume you've got a trolley jack. The next question is - where to stick it? If you put the jack under the sill, you can't add an axle stand later. An alternative front jacking point is the rear mounting points of the front suspension lower arms - jack up under there (with a nice flat offcut of wood on your jack head), and pop an axle stand (also with block of wood if poss) under the sill jacking point, marked by two little notches in the sill edge, or by an arrowhead marking. With the stand in place, you can lower the jack so the car's weight rests on the stand. We prefer to spread the weight between the stands and the jack, so don't lower the jack completely, unless you're jacking up the other side too.

Don't jack up the car, or stick stands under the car, anywhere other than kosher jacking and support points. This means - not the floorpan or the sump (you'll cave it in), not the suspension bits (not stable), and not under the brake/fuel pipes.

Jacking up the rear

When jacking up the rear of the car, place wooden chocks in front of the front wheels to stop it rolling forwards, and engage first gear.

If you're taking the wheels off, loosen the rear wheel bolts with the wheels on the ground.

To raise both rear wheels off the ground at the same time, you'll have to remove the spare wheel from its cradle to gain access to the rear crossmember. The rear of the car can then safely be lifted using a hydraulic jack positioned under the centre point of the rear crossmember (not the axle). With the vehicle raised, position an axle stand and block of wood beneath the rear jacking point on each sill. Set both stands to the required height, then slowly lower the jack whilst aligning the stand block slots with the lower lip of each sill. Ensure both stands are correctly positioned before removing the jack completely.

Remember not to put your axle stands under any pipes, or the fuel tank, and you should live to see another Christmas.

Finally...

As far as possible, don't leave the car unattended once it has been lifted; if it falls and hurts someone it would almost certainly be your fault.

Combination of trolley jack and axle stand around the rear sill jacking point.

Trolley jack under the rear crossmember, to lift both rear wheels off the deck.

Tricks 'n' tips

Whenever you have your wheels off, clean off any hub corrosion with wet-and-dry paper, then coat the hub mating surfaces with copper (brake) grease - this "sticks" better than ordinary grease, and is temperature-resistant. There's no way you'll suffer stuck-on wheels again. "Proper" alloys come with a plastic collar which fits inside the wheel - this is an essential item which should not be discarded, as it centres the wheel properly and reduces wheel-to-hub corrosion.

Changing wheels

Before fitting your new wheels, there's stuff to check - first, have you got a plastic ring inside the hub (spigot)? Without it the wheel won't centre properly. It could cause damage to the bolts.

Always tighten the wheel bolts securely (ideally, to the correct torque - Citroën's figure is 85 Nm, but check with your wheel manufacturer). This can only be done properly with the wheel back on the ground. Don't over-tighten the bolts, or you'll never get them undone at the roadside, should you have a flat. If your wheels have a centre cap of some kind, make sure you fit it. Not only does it look better, but in certain cases, the Allen key needed to undo it might be all the theft-deterrent you need, to stop an opportunist...

Pop the wheel on, turning it to align the bolt holes, then in with the nicely-greased bolts, and tighten up as far as possible by hand. On the fronts (unless you've left it in gear) you won't be able to fully tighten the bolts anyway, as the wheels will spin. Keep your locking wheel bolt tool somewhere safe, but not obvious.

You'll be doing yourself a favour if some of the same copper grease also finds its way onto the wheel bolt threads. Make sure the bolts are long enough to bite into the hub sufficiently.

Equip yourself with some copper brake grease, and smear some on the wheel boss, inside.

01 Equip yourself with some copper brake grease, and smear some on the wheel boss, inside.

02 You'll be doing yourself a favour if some of the same copper grease also finds its way onto the wheel bolt threads. Make sure the bolts are long enough to bite into the hub sufficiently.

03 Pop the wheel on... Keep your locking wheel bolt tool somewhere safe, but not obvious.

04 ...to stop an opportunist...

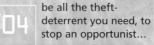

Tricks 'n' tips
When buying tyres, look out for black round ones, they tend to handle better. Some also feature a rubbing strip on the sidewall - these extend over the edge of the wheel rims, and the idea is that they protect the rim edges from damage by "kerbing". Our Toyo Proxes had these strips - discreet and very practical, we reckon.

Tyres

Tyres are the only thing keeping your car contact with the road, so it figures that they're one of the most important components of your car. Saving a tenner (or more) a tyre might feel good when you pay the bill, but will you still feel the same way, the first time you blast down your favourite stretch of road, only to find yourself heading for a hedge mid-corner?

Choosing a known brand of tyre will prove to be one of your better decisions. Tyres are the only thing keeping you on the road, as in steering, braking and helping you round corners - what's the point of trying to improve the handling by fitting a quality suspension kit if you're going to throw the gains away by fitting naff tyres? Why beef up the brakes if the tyres won't bite? The combination of stiff suspension and cheap tyres is inherently dangerous - because the front end dives less with reduced suspension travel, the front tyres are far more likely to lock and skid under heavy braking. A problem with really wide tyres is aquaplaning - hit a big puddle at speed, and the tyre skates over the water without gripping - this is seriously scary when it first happens. Fitting good tyres won't prevent it, but it might increase your chances of staying in control. When choosing tyres listen to friends and fellow modifiers - real-world experience counts for a lot when choosing tyres (how well do they grip, wet or dry? How many miles can you get out of them?) Just make sure, before you spend your money on decent tyres, that you've cured all your rubbing and scrubbing issues, as nothing will rip your new tyres out faster.

Tricks 'n' tips
If you're buying a new set of wheels, most centres will offer you options on various set of tyres which they'll fit for you. Not only is this convenient, but it's usually top value too.

Marks on your sidewalls

Tyre sizes are expressed in a strange mixture of metric and imperial specs - we'll take a typical tyre size as an example:

205/40 R 17 V

for a 7-inch wide 17-inch rim

205 width of tyre in millimetres

40 this is the "aspect ratio" (or "profile") of the tyre, or the sidewall height in relation to tyre width, expressed as a percentage, in this case 40%. So - 40% of 205 mm = 82 mm, or the height of the tyre sidewall from the edge of the locating bead to the top of the tread.

R Radial.

17 Wheel diameter in inches.

V Speed rating (in this case, suitable for use up to 150 mph).

Not only is it essential to ensure the tyre is the right size for the rim, but the speed rating must also be suitable for the car. Tyres with an insufficient speed rating mean an MOT failure. This isn't a major problem on a base-model Saxo, but if you've got a VTR or VTS, ensure all tyres fitted have at least a V rating (not that you'd consider fitting anything less anyway).

Pressure situation

Don't forget, when you're having your new tyres fitted, to ask what the recommended pressures should be, front and rear - it's unlikely that the Citroën specs for this will be relevant to your new low-low profiles, but it's somewhere to start from. If the guy fitting your tyres is no help on this point, contact the tyre manufacturer - the big ones might even have a half-useful website. Running the tyres at the wrong pressures is a bad idea (you'll stand to wear them out much faster) and can be very dangerous (too soft - tyre rolls off the rim, too hard - tyre slides, no grip).

Speed ratings

Besides the tyre size, tyres are marked with a maximum speed rating, expressed as a letter code:

T   up to 190 km/h (118 mph)

U   up to 200 km/h (124 mph)

H   up to 210 km/h (130 mph)

V   inside tyre size markings (225/50 VR 16) over 210 km/h (130 mph)

V   outside tyre size markings (185/55 R 15 V) up to 240 km/h (150 mph)

Z   inside tyre size markings (255/40 ZR 17) over 240 km/h (150 mph)

08 Suspension

If your Saxo's still sitting on standard suspension, it's probably safe to say it doesn't cut it - yet. If you've decided you couldn't wait to fit your big alloys, the chances are your Saxo is now doing a passable impression of a tractor. Lowering the suspension is the only option then - so how low do you go, and what side-effects will a lowering kit have?

As for what to buy, there are basically three main options when it comes to lowering the front, arranged in order of ascending cost below:

1 *Set of lowering springs*

2 *Matched set of lowering springs and shock absorbers*

3 *Set of "coilovers"*

One reason for lowering is, of course, to make your car look cool. Standard suspension nearly always seems to be set too soft and too high - a nicely lowered motor stands out instantly. Lowering your car should also improve the handling. Dropping the car on its suspension brings the car's centre of gravity closer to its roll and pitch centres, which helps to pin it to the road in corners and under braking - combined with stiffer springs and shocks, this reduces body roll and increases the tyre contact patch on the road. But - if improving the handling is really important to you, choose your new suspension carefully. If you go the cheap route, or want extreme lowering, then making the car handle better might not be what you achieve…

How low to go?

Assuming you want to slam your suspension so that your arches just clear the tops of your rims, there's another small problem - it takes some inspired guesswork (or hours of careful measuring and head-scratching) to assess the required drop accurately, and avoid that nasty rubbing sound. Lowering springs and suspension kits will only produce a fixed amount of drop - this can range from 20 mm to a more extreme drop of anything up to 80 mm. Take as many measurements as possible, and ask around your mates - although suppliers and manufacturers may be your best source of help in special cases. Coilovers have a range of adjustment possible, which is far more satisfactory - at a price.

Torsion bars

Sorry to start on a negative note, but lowering the rear-end of your Saxo properly really is a job for a professional. The reason for this is the manufacturer's choice of rear suspension - the Saxo is fitted with a torsion bar rear axle (a favourite choice amongst the French manufacturers).

The torsion bar rear suspension doesn't use coil springs, but instead uses hefty steel bars. The steel bars are splined at each end, and link each trailing arm to the opposite end of the axle crossmember; one is positioned in front of the crossmember and the other behind it. These steel bars twist as the suspension moves up and down throughout its travel, and it's the bars' resistance to this twisting (or torsional force) which provides the rear suspension springing. Another steel bar passes through the centre of the rear axle crossmember and links both trailing arms - this is the anti-roll bar, which is stiffer than the other two, but otherwise functions on the same principle.

Resetting the rear ride height is an involved procedure - not especially difficult or dangerous, but fiddly (and you could be playing for a long time before giving up and taking it to a garage). On an older car, you could also be facing the possibility of rusted-in bits, and a slide-hammer is the only answer if you get into that. The positive side though, is that you can lower the rear ride height without purchasing any new springs - the only cost involved is the labour.

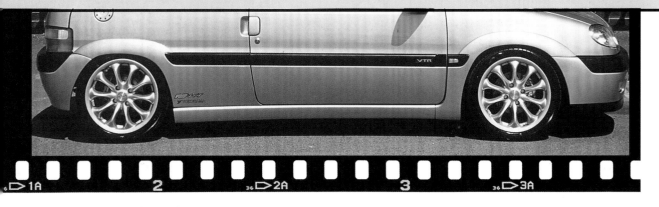

Lowering
Rear
suspension

The adjustment procedure involves removing the torsion bars, setting both trailing arms to the correct height, then re-inserting the bars, ensuring their splines are correctly engaged. Sounds easy when you say it quickly, but it might not be when you try it. Here's a rough guide to how the experts do it:

01 Jack up the rear of the car and remove the rear wheels.

02 Remove the anti-roll bar plates (one on each side) and remove the anti-roll bar.

Remove the damper unit and fit an adjustable dummy damper (which is set at the required height) to the car.

03

Unscrew and remove the cover from the torsion bars (one on each side).

04

One at a time (driver's-side first) remove the torsion bar, turn it anti-clockwise one spline and re-insert it. On the passenger side, the torsion bar needs to be turned one spline clockwise.

05 Refit all your bits including the anti-roll bar.

06 Now you can fit your new dampers.

Lowering

Front suspension

Lowering springs - cheap and cheerful

The cheapest option by far. Lowering springs are, effectively, shorter versions of the standard items fitted to your Saxo at the factory. However, not only are they shorter (lower), they are also of necessity uprated (stiffer) - if lowering springs were simply shorter than standard and the same stiffness ("rate"), you'd be hitting the bump-stops over every set of catseyes. With just a set of lowering springs, you fit new springs and keep the original shock absorbers (or dampers). Even if the originals are in good condition, you can see just fitting a set of uprated springs is a bit of a compromise. The original dampers were carefully chosen to work in harmony with the original springs - by uprating the springs without changing the dampers, you end up with a situation where the dampers and springs are mis-matched.

Fitting lowering springs will have the desired effect on the appearance of the car, but the mis-matched springs and dampers could adversely effect the handling. A very hard and choppy ride are well-documented problems associated with taking the cheap option. If you drive your car hard, bear this in mind. You'd be much better off going for a full suspension kit with matched dampers and springs, which will ensure predicable handling. If the cost prohibits this and lowering springs are the only option for now, at least buy branded items of decent quality.

Fitting lowering springs

Quite an involved procedure this, and you'll need the correct tools for the job. A set of coil spring compressors is essential equipment - no way can you dismantle the struts safely without them. A balljoint separator will probably be needed to disconnect the steering track rod balljoints. If you haven't got a set of spring compressors and can't beg/steal/borrow some, you ought to leave this one to the professionals. If you want to, to save a bit of cash, you could still remove the struts yourself, and just have them stripped and rebuilt by a garage.

If you've got the tools, the procedure is almost identical to fitting a full kit, the difference being that you are not fitting new damper cartridges in the strut, so follow the procedure but ignore the bits to do with the damper unit.

Suspension kit

A full suspension kit is a genuine upgrade, so with a properly-sorted conversion you'll get the required drop but still retain predictable handling characteristics. With a matched set of lowered springs and uprated dampers, improved handling is assured, and the ride quality should remain smooth yet taut. Some of the kits are billed as "adjustable", but this only applies to the damper rates, and not the ride height.

Attention!
Changing the damper cartridges presents a problem. The cartridge is retained by a nut which requires a special peg spanner to slacken/tighten it. Without the special peg spanner, removing the nut will be tricky, since it's done up very tight.

Jack up the front of the car and remove both front roadwheels (see "Wheels & tyres"). Using a hammer and pointed-nose chisel, relieve the staking on each driveshaft nut. Take note of how the nut is staked in place (this stops it coming undone) - you'll need to stake the new nut in place the same way.

01

When it comes to the driveshaft nut, use decent-quality tools which fit the nut properly, and support the car with a jack and axle stands. The driveshaft nut is really, really tight, and serious force will be needed to move it - don't take chances with dodgy equipment. Oh, and a new nut will be needed on refitting.

02

If the anti-roll bar is connected to the strut, unscrew the nut and washer and disconnect the anti-roll bar connecting link from the strut body. If the anti-roll bar is connected to the lower arm, unscrew the bolts and washers and remove the mounting clamp from the top of the lower arm. If necessary, also remove the rubber bush from the bar end.

03

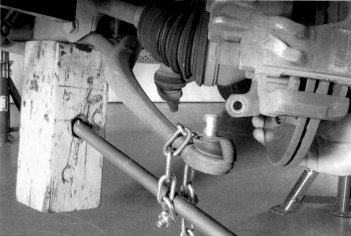

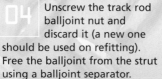

04 Unscrew the track rod balljoint nut and discard it (a new one should be used on refitting). Free the balljoint from the strut using a balljoint separator.

05 Unscrew the nut and remove the lower arm balljoint clamp bolt from the base of the hub carrier. Discard the nut (a new one should be used on refitting).

06 Lever down the lower arm, taking care not to damage the balljoint gaiter, just enough to release the balljoint from the hub carrier. As you can see we used a chain, block of wood and a metal bar to create a levering device. If the balljoint is a tight fit, open up the hub carrier clamp a little. Once the balljoint is free, position the strut clear then release the lower arm. Don't lose the protector plate from the lower arm balljoint.

07 Release the hub assembly from the driveshaft by pulling the strut/hub carrier outwards. If necessary, the driveshaft can be tapped out of the hub using a soft-faced hammer. Support the driveshaft by resting it on the lower arm or tying it to the car body. Don't allow it to hang down, as this could damage the driveshaft joints and gaiters. Ensure the brake hose and any relevant wiring is released from the strut/hub carrier.

08 Slacken and remove the bolts securing the caliper/mounting bracket to the hub assembly (Citroën recommend these bolts should be renewed everytime they are removed). On models with solid brake discs, note the following: a) On the ATE/Teves caliper, it will be necessary to remove the cap to gain access to the lower bolt. b) On the Bendix/Bosch caliper, note the correct position of the retaining plate fitted to the mounting bolts.

09 Slide the brake caliper off the disc, and tie it to the car body to support it. Don't allow it to hang by the flexible hose as this will strain and damage the hose. On models with ABS, unscrew the nut and remove the protective shield from the sensor. Unscrew the sensor bolt then free the sensor from the hub carrier and position it clear so it will not get damaged during strut removal.

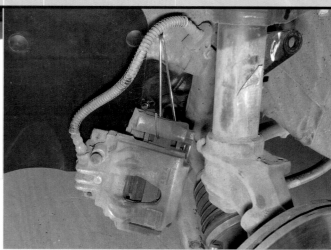

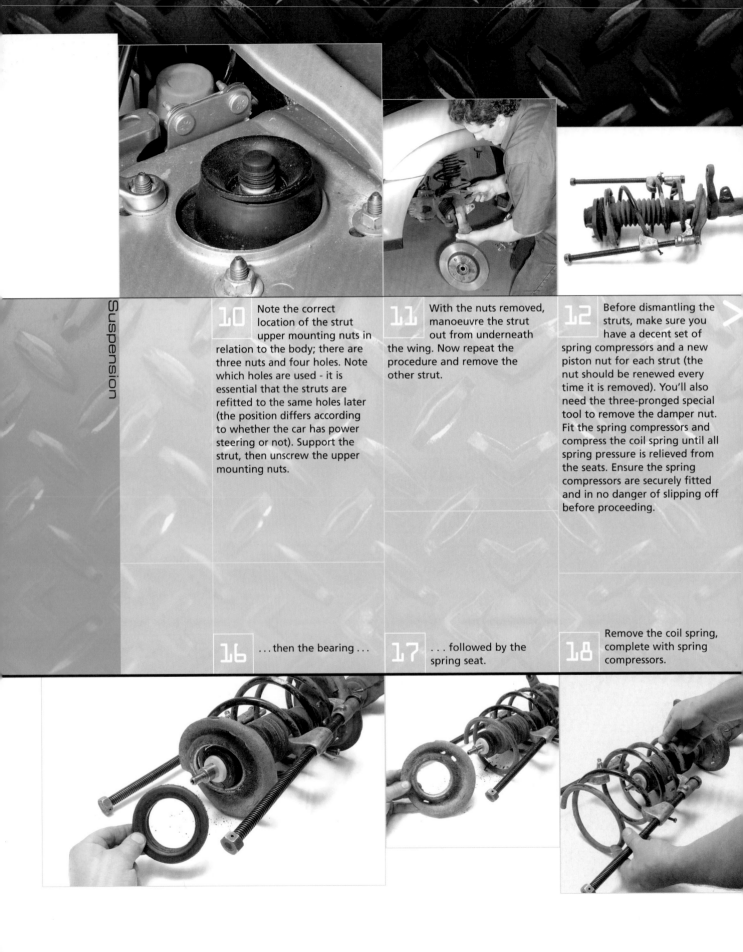

10 Note the correct location of the strut upper mounting nuts in relation to the body; there are three nuts and four holes. Note which holes are used - it is essential that the struts are refitted to the same holes later (the position differs according to whether the car has power steering or not). Support the strut, then unscrew the upper mounting nuts.

11 With the nuts removed, manoeuvre the strut out from underneath the wing. Now repeat the procedure and remove the other strut.

12 Before dismantling the struts, make sure you have a decent set of spring compressors and a new piston nut for each strut (the nut should be renewed every time it is removed). You'll also need the three-pronged special tool to remove the damper nut. Fit the spring compressors and compress the coil spring until all spring pressure is relieved from the seats. Ensure the spring compressors are securely fitted and in no danger of slipping off before proceeding.

16 . . . then the bearing . . .

17 . . . followed by the spring seat.

18 Remove the coil spring, complete with spring compressors.

13 Remove the trim cap, then slacken and remove the piston nut and its collar. If necessary, retain the piston with a Torx/Allen key (ours was a T40 Torx) to prevent rotation whilst slackening the nut. Discard the nut (a new one should be fitted).

14 Lift off the strut upper mounting plate . . .

15 . . . followed by the bearing top plate . . .

19 Slide the rubber gaiter off the strut . . .

20 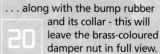 . . . along with the bump rubber and its collar - this will leave the brass-coloured damper nut in full view.

21 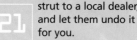 To remove the damper nut you need a special tool, as mentioned earlier. If you do not have access to this tool, it might be worth taking your strut to a local dealer, and let them undo it for you.

22 Remove the old damper and fit the new one. Take your new damper with you to your dealer, because you may as well get them to do the nut up for you, too.

23 Now extend the new damper fully.

27 Fit the bearing to the centre of the upper seat.

28 Locate the bearing top plate on the top of the bearing . . .

29 . . . and fit the upper mounting plate.

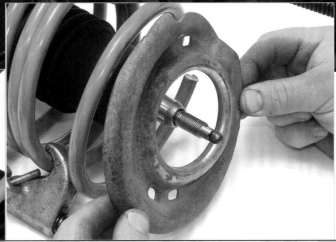

24 Ensure the rubber collar and bump stop are in position on the damper piston, then seat the rubber gaiter on the strut body.

25 Carefully release the spring compressors from the old springs, and transfer them to the new springs. Compress the spring sufficiently to allow the strut to be reassembled. Fit the compressed new spring onto the strut, and locate its lower end up against the stop on the lower seat.

26 Fit the upper seat to the spring, positioning its stop against the spring upper end.

Insert the dished collar, then screw the new nut onto the piston. Retain the piston and tighten the nut to 70 Nm. Fit the trim cap to the piston end. **30**

Ensure the spring upper and lower ends are correctly located against the stops on the seats, then carefully release the spring compressors. Remove the compressors and check that all components are correctly seated. Ensure the upper end of the rubber gaiter is pushed firmly up into the base of the lower seat, and the gaiter lower end is correctly seated on the strut body before fitting the strut to the car. **31**

Refitting the strut is basically the reverse of removal, but listed below are the tightening torques for the various bits. After messing with your suspension, make sure that you get the wheel alignment checked - especially camber and tracking. If you don't, you may have curious handling, strange steering, and tyres which seem to disappear overnight (see "Nasty side-effects"). **32**

Three strut mounting nuts	**20** Nm
Lower arm balljoint clamp bolt	**38** Nm
Track rod balljoint nut	**35** Nm
Anti-roll bar to lower arm	**25** Nm
Anti-roll bar to strut	**70** Nm
Driveshaft nuts (stake in place when tight)	**250** Nm
Caliper bolts:	
Solid discs with ATE/Teves calipers:	
M8 bolt	**35** Nm
M12 bolt	**105** Nm
Solid disc with Bendix /Bosch calipers	**120** Nm
Ventilated discs	**120** Nm

Coilovers

If you've chosen coilovers - you obviously know quality when you see it, and you're not prepared to compromise. True, quality costs, but you get what you pay for. This is the most expensive option, but it offers one vital feature that the other two can't - true adjustability of ride height (at the front). This means that you can make the finest of tweaks to lower your car over your rims. This also gives you more scope to fit those big rims now, lower it down as far as poss, then wait 'til next month before you have the arches rolled, and drop it down to the deck. Coilovers are a variation on the suspension kit theme, in that they are a set of matched springs and dampers, but with the added bonus of being fully adjustable (within certain limits, obviously).

Coilover conversion

Another option gaining ground is the "coilover conversion". If you must have the lowest, baddest machine, and don't care what the ride will be like, these could be the answer. Offering as much potential for lowering as genuine coilovers (and at far less cost), these items could be described as a cross between coilovers and lowering springs - the standard dampers are retained (this is one reason why the ride suffers). What you get is a new spring assembly, with adjustable top and bottom mounts - the whole thing slips over your standard damper. Two problems with this solution:

1 Standard dampers won't be able to cope with the uprated springs, so the car will ride (and handle) like a pig if you go for a really serious drop - and why else would you be doing it?

2 The standard dampers are effectively being compressed, the lower you go. There is a limit to how far they will compress before being completely solid (and this is the limit for your lowering activities). Needless to say, even a partly-compressed damper won't be able to do much actual damping - the results could be… interesting…

Nasty
side-effects

Camber angle and tracking

With any lowering "solution", your suspension and steering geometry will be affected - this will be more of a problem the lower you go. This will manifest itself as steering which either becomes lighter or (more usually) heavier, and as tyres which scrub out their inner or outer edges in very short order - not funny, if you're running expensive low-profiles. Sometimes even the rear tyres can be affected in this way, but that's usually only after some serious slammage. Whenever you've fitted a set of springs (and this applies to all types), have the geometry checked ASAP afterwards.

Rear brake pressure regulator

Some Saxos have a rear brake pressure limiting valve fitted, which is linked to the rear suspension. When the car's lightly loaded over the rear wheels, the braking effort to the rear is limited, to prevent the wheels locking up. With the boot full of luggage, the back end sinks down, and the valve lets full braking pressure through to the rear. When you slam the suspension, the valve is fooled into thinking the car's loaded up, and you might find the rear brakes locking up unexpectedly - could be a nasty surprise on a wet roundabout.

The valves aren't generally intended to be easy to adjust, but they are quite simple devices - the best idea would be to get underneath and see how it looks when sat on its wheels unloaded (on standard suspension), and try to re-create the same condition once the car's been dropped. You're looking for a bracket bolted to the rear "axle", with a small spring attached.

Strut brace

Another race inspired item is the strut brace. The idea of the strut brace is that, once you've stiffened up your front suspension to the max, the car's body shell (to which the front suspension struts are bolted) may not be able to cope with the cornering forces being put through it, and will flex, leading to unsatisfactory handling.

The strut brace (in theory) does exactly what it says on the tin, by providing support between the strut tops, taking the load off the bodyshell. The strut brace may indeed have a slight effect, but the real reason to fit one is for show Strut braces can be chromed, painted or anodised, and can be fitted with matching chromed/coloured strut top plates.

01 Our strut brace came in red - but we didn't want that on our silver Saxo, so we re-sprayed it. If you decide to do the same, remember to mask up the threaded adjuster section before you start.

02 Hanging the brace up by one of the mounting holes will make spraying it a whole lot easier.

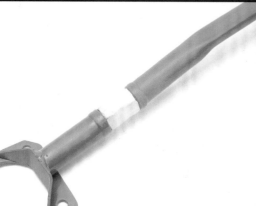

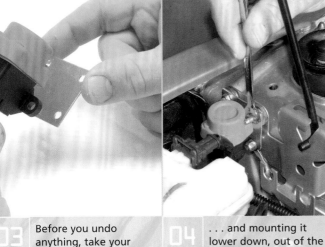

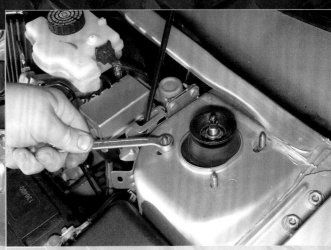

03 Before you undo anything, take your strut brace and offer it into position. You may find straight away that you have to remount the fuel cut-off inertia switch (the bright red thing next to the passenger-side strut top). It's only a case of unbolting it, making up a new mounting bracket . . .

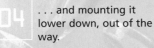

04 . . . and mounting it lower down, out of the way.

05 With the car resting on its wheels, remove the three suspension strut upper mounting nuts from each side of the engine compartment.

Now tighten the strut brace itself, to set the "tension" - don't try too hard with this, just take up the slack and a bit more. Use a screwdriver through the hole in the threaded section to hold it while the large nuts either side are done up.

Place the strut brace into position, and refit the mounting nuts, leaving them loose at this stage.

06

Now tighten the three nuts on each strut top mount - if you've got a torque wrench, set it to 20 Nm.

07

Brakes

The middle pedal

Car makers realise that stopping quickly is of the utmost importance, and as such the Saxo is equipped with a reasonable set of stoppers. That said, those of you without the all-disc VTR/VTS setup might still yearn for more anchorage.

Brake mods can range from simply colour-coding your calipers and drums to fitting uprated front discs and pads. As the front brakes do the most of the donkey work when braking, it's probably only worth upgrading the front brakes, and not really bothering much about the rears. That being said, you could consider replacing those puny non-VTR/S rear brake drums with a rear disc brake conversion.

If you're uprating your brakes in any major way, then let your insurance company know (see "Insurance" section).

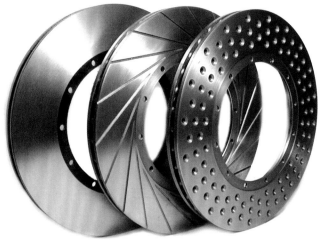

Performance discs

Besides the various brands of performance brake pads that go with them, the main brake upgrade is to fit performance front brake discs and pads. Discs are available in two main types - grooved and cross-drilled.

Grooved discs (which can be had with varying numbers of grooves) serve a dual purpose - the grooves provide a "channel" to help the heat escape, and they also help to de-glaze the pad surface, cleaning up the pads every time they're used. Some of the discs are made from higher-friction metal than normal discs, too, and the fact that they improve braking performance is well-documented.

Cross-drilled discs offer another route to heat dissipation, but one which can present some problems. Some of these discs can crack around the drilled holes after serious use. The trouble is that the heat "migrates" to the drilled holes (as was intended), but the heat build-up can be extreme, and the constant heating/cooling cycle can stress the metal to the point where it will crack. Discs which have been damaged in this way are extremely dangerous as they could break up completely at any time. Only fit discs of this type from established manufacturers offering a guarantee of quality, and check the discs regularly.

Performance discs also have a reputation for warping (nasty vibrations felt through the pedal). Now this may be so, but of course, the harder you use your brakes (and ones you've uprated may well get serious abuse), the greater the heat you'll generate. Cheap discs, or ones which have had a hard time over umpteen thousands of miles, probably will warp. So buy quality, and don't get too heroic on the brakes for too long.

Performance pads can be fitted to any brake discs, including the standard ones, but are of course designed to work best with heat-dissipating discs. Unless your Saxo's got a supercharged, turbocharged 16-valve nutter of an engine under the bonnet, don't be tempted to go much further than "fast road" pads - anything more competition-orientated may take too long to come up to temperature on the road, and might leave you with less braking than before.

Lastly, fitting all the performance brake bits in the world is no use if your calipers have seized up. If, when you strip out your old pads, you find that one pad's worn more than the other, or that both pads have worn more on the left wheel than the right, your caliper pistons are sticking. Sometimes you can free them off by pushing them back into the caliper, but this could be a garage job to fix. If you drive around with sticking calipers, you'll eat pads and discs. Your choice.

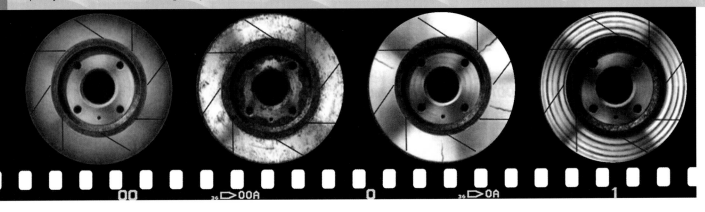

Painting
calipers

One downside to fitting big alloys is that it exposes your standard brakes. One option is to paint some of the brake parts so they look nicer (red is common, but isn't the only choice). Only the VTR and VTS have rear discs, but painting the brake drums is acceptable. Painting the calipers requires that they're really clean. Accessory stores sell aerosol brake cleaner for removing brake dust. Some kits come complete with cleaner spray.

01 We know you won't necessarily want to hear this, but the best way to paint the calipers is to do some dismantling first. The kits say you don't have to, but you'll get a much better result from a few minutes' extra work. Remove the calipers as described in the brake pad section. You don't have to detach the brake hoses, but make sure that you support the calipers so that the hose is not under strain. Clean the calipers using brake cleaner, making sure that you remove all the dirt and muck.

Attention!
If you disconnect the brake caliper hose, you'll have to bleed the brake hydraulic system afterwards, otherwise the brakes won't work. You'll also be mopping up spills of brake fluid, which is nasty stuff. See your Haynes manual for details.

02 Remove the caliper mounting bracket as described in the brake disc section. Again, clean it thoroughly using brake cleaner, followed by a wire brush.

03 Carefully paint the mounting bracket and caliper body. make sure you don't get paint on areas where pads, discs or piston touch. Don't paint the caliper piston. Allow to dry and apply a second coat if required. Refit your bits.

Tricks 'n' tips
If you have trouble reassembling your brakes after painting, you probably got carried away and put on too much paint. We found that, once it was fully dry, the excess paint could be trimmed off with a knife.

Attention!
Brake dust from old pads may contain asbestos. Wear a mask to avoid inhaling it. Dispose of old brake system components safely at your local waste recycling centre - don't just put them in the bin.

Front
brake pads

Fitting pads is simple and straightforward operation; it doesn't matter what type of pads you buy, installation is the same for all makes. One area of confusion though, may be obtaining the correct type of pads; the Saxo has three different types of front brake caliper. Make sure you state the exact make and model when purchasing pads, and check they are the right sort before wasting your time removing the originals. If you're unsure "ventilated" discs are the ones with "holes" in the edges - only fitted to Saxos of the VTR and VTS persuasion.

Remember 1 - It's a good idea to have your brake mods MOT-tested once you've fitted new discs and pads, and you might even be able to "blag" a free brake check at your local fast-fit centre if you're crafty. Brakes are a serious safety issue, and unless you're 100% confident that all is well, demo-ing your car's awesome new-found stopping ability could find you in the ditch...
Remember 2 - New pads of any sort need careful bedding-in before they'll work properly - when first fitted, the pad surface won't have worn exactly to the contours of the disc, so it won't actually be touching it over its full area. Especially true when new pads are fitted to worn discs. It is vital to follow the bedding-in instructions, and not get the brakes very hot until after you've driven a good hundred miles.

Bendix/Bosch caliper
solid discs

01 Jack up the car and remove both front wheels (see "Wheels & tyres"). Note the fitted positions of the pad springs, the retaining plate and spring clip.

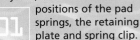

02 Using pliers, remove the spring clip from the pad retaining plate . . .

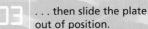

03 . . . then slide the plate out of position.

This caliper is generally only fitted to Saxos up to 1.4 litres, without power steering - but it's best to check before laying out on new bits.

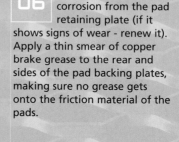

04 Slide the original pads complete with their pad springs out from the caliper. Remove the spring from each pad, noting its correct fitted location.

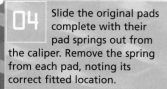

05 If the old pads are well worn, you'll need to push the piston back into the caliper to make room for your new pads. Do this either with a G-clamp or a pair of grips, or alternatively by levering the caliper outwards using a piece of wood. As you push the piston back in, watch the fluid level in the reservoir. If the fluid level rises above the "MAXI" level line, siphon out the excess with a syringe. Don't siphon it by mouth, as the fluid is poisonous.

06 Remove all traces of corrosion from the pad retaining plate (if it shows signs of wear - renew it). Apply a thin smear of copper brake grease to the rear and sides of the pad backing plates, making sure no grease gets onto the friction material of the pads.

Fit the pad springs correctly to the new pads. The springs must be fitted so that when the pads are installed in the caliper, they will be located at the opposite end to the retaining plate. Insert the pads, complete with pad springs, into the caliper, ensuring the friction material of each one is facing the brake disc.

07

Ensure the pads and spring are correctly located in the caliper . . .

08

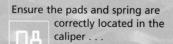

. . . then slide the retaining plate into position (give this a little copper grease, too) and secure it in position with the spring clip.

09

Repeat the procedure on the opposite side. With both sets of pads correctly fitted, repeatedly press the brake pedal to force the pads onto the discs. Refit the wheels then lower the car to the ground. Before driving the car, check the brake fluid level. Remember the pads will need to "bed-in", so take it easy for the first 100 miles or so.

10

ATE/Teves
FR12 caliper
solid discs

Our Saxo didn't have this caliper, but they are out there. In case your car has these "unpopular" calipers, here's the basic procedure. According to our files, this caliper's fitted to models up to 1.4 litres, with power steering - if that helps.

Jack up the car and remove both front wheels (see "Wheels & tyres"). Before going any further, take a good look at the position of the pad spring, and memorise its correct fitted location.

Using a hammer and pin punch, tap the pad retaining pins out from the caliper, and remove the pad spring. Slide the original pads and their backing shims (where fitted) out from the caliper.

If the old pads are well worn, you'll need to push the piston back into the caliper to make room for your all that extra friction material. Do this either with a G-clamp or a pair of grips, or alternatively by levering the caliper outwards using a piece of wood. As you're pushing the piston back in, watch the fluid level in the reservoir. If the fluid level rises above the "MAXI" level line, siphon out the excess with a syringe. Don't siphon it by mouth, as the fluid is poisonous.

Remove all traces of corrosion from the pad retaining pins (if they show signs of wear - renew them) then apply a thin smear of copper brake grease to each pin. Also apply a thin smear to the rear and sides of the pad backing plates. Take care to make sure no grease gets onto the friction material of the pads.

Insert the pads, complete with backing shims (where fitted), into the caliper ensuring the friction material of each one is facing the brake disc. Locate the pad spring on the top of the pads, and insert both retaining pins. Tap the lower pin into position, ensuring it passes through both pad holes and the centre of the spring. With the lower pin in position, tap in the upper pin through both pads and over the top of the spring ends.

Repeat the procedure on the opposite side. With both sets of pads correctly fitted, repeatedly press the brake pedal to force the pads onto the discs. Refit the wheels, then lower the car to the ground. Before driving the car, check the brake fluid level. Remember the pads will need to "bed-in", so take it easy for the first 100 miles or so.

ATE/Teves
FN48 caliper
ventilated discs

01. Jack up the front of the car and remove both front roadwheels (see "Wheels & tyres"). Note the correct fitted location of the pad spring then, using a flat-bladed screwdriver, carefully prise the spring out of position and remove it from the caliper.

02 Remove the two caps from the inner edge of the caliper to gain access to the guide pin bolts.

03 Unscrew both guide pin bolts.

04 Slide the caliper assembly off the brake disc, then unclip the inner pad from the caliper piston. Don't allow the caliper to hang from the brake hose (this will damage the hose); tie it to the suspension strut.

05 Remove the outer pad from the caliper mounting bracket.

06 If the originals are well worn, you'll need to push the piston back into the caliper to make room for all that extra friction material. Do this either with a G-clamp or a pair of grips or alternatively by levering it back using a piece of wood. As you're pushing the piston back in, keep an eye on the fluid level in the master cylinder reservoir. If the fluid level rises above the "MAXI" level line, siphon out the excess with a syringe. Don't siphon it by mouth, as the fluid is poisonous.

07 Remove all traces of corrosion from the caliper mounting bracket, then apply a thin smear of copper-based brake grease to the rear and sides of the pad backing plates. Take care to make sure no grease gets onto the friction material of the pads. Also smear copper grease into the grooves where the pads rest. Where'd that new disc come from?

08 Clip the new inner pad into position in the caliper piston and fit the outer pad to the mounting bracket ensuring its friction material is facing the brake disc.

Repeat the procedure on the opposite side. With both sets of pads correctly fitted, repeatedly press the brake pedal to force the pads onto the discs. Refit the wheels, then lower the car to the ground. Before driving the car, check the brake fluid level. Remember the pads will need to "bed-in", so take it easy for the first 100 miles or so.

09 Slide the caliper and inner pad into position, and align it with the mounting bracket.

10 Lightly grease and refit the guide mounting bolts, tighten them to the correct torque (27 Nm), then securely fit the bolt caps.

11 Fit the pad spring to the caliper, ensuring its ends are correctly hooked in the caliper holes.

12

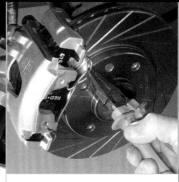

Front brake discs

Performance discs are available in two main types - grooved and cross-drilled (and a combination of both). Both perform similarly and offer the same advantages, so the decision is down to you

Fitting discs is simple and straightforward operation and installation is the same for all makes. Make sure you state the exact make and model when purchasing discs, and check they are the right diameter before wasting your time removing the originals. And always fit new pads at the same time.

01 Jack up the front of the car and remove both front wheels (see "Wheels & tyres"). Remove the original brake pads as described earlier. On models with ventilated discs, slacken and remove the two bolts and remove the brake caliper mounting bracket from the hub (Citroën say that new bolts must be used on refitting, and we're inclined to agree - they're done up very tight).

02 All that holds the disc in place (apart from the wheel bolts, when the wheel's on) is one or two screws. They are frequently very rusty and hard to remove.

If so, a good clout with a hammer (and a soak with WD-40) might free off a rusted-in screw, but an impact driver or even a drill may be needed. Ours came off with no effort...

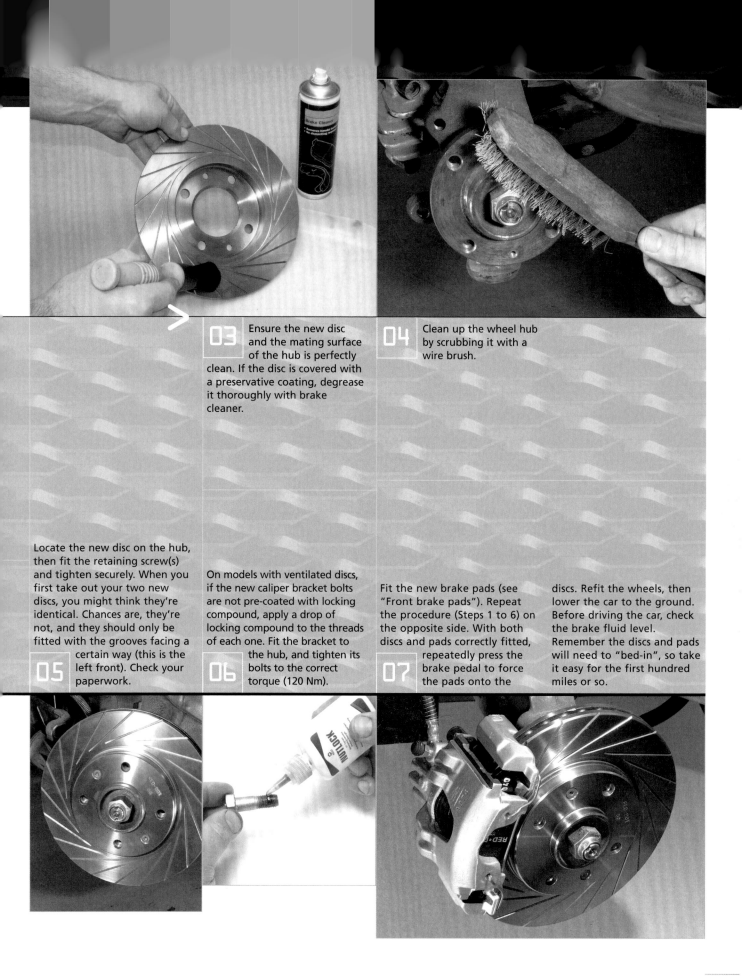

03 Ensure the new disc and the mating surface of the hub is perfectly clean. If the disc is covered with a preservative coating, degrease it thoroughly with brake cleaner.

04 Clean up the wheel hub by scrubbing it with a wire brush.

05 Locate the new disc on the hub, then fit the retaining screw(s) and tighten securely. When you first take out your two new discs, you might think they're identical. Chances are, they're not, and they should only be fitted with the grooves facing a certain way (this is the left front). Check your paperwork.

06 On models with ventilated discs, if the new caliper bracket bolts are not pre-coated with locking compound, apply a drop of locking compound to the threads of each one. Fit the bracket to the hub, and tighten its bolts to the correct torque (120 Nm).

07 Fit the new brake pads (see "Front brake pads"). Repeat the procedure (Steps 1 to 6) on the opposite side. With both discs and pads correctly fitted, repeatedly press the brake pedal to force the pads onto the discs. Refit the wheels, then lower the car to the ground. Before driving the car, check the brake fluid level. Remember the discs and pads will need to "bed-in", so take it easy for the first hundred miles or so.

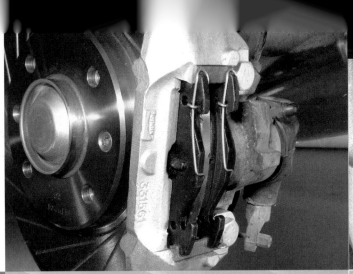

Rear disc brakes

This procedure covers changing the pads and discs together, so you won't have to do ALL this if you only want to change the pads. Read it through before you start, though.

01 Jack up the rear of the car, and remove both rear wheels (see "Wheels & tyres"). Extract the tiny little spring clip from the pad retaining plate. Citroën stage you must fit a new spring clip when refitting - you'll probably need a new one anyway, once the original flies off and gets lost!

02 Slide the pad retaining plate out of the caliper.

07 Clean up the wheel hub by scrubbing it with a wire brush. It's vital to get the hub face as clean as possible. Any traces of dirt could prevent the disc from mating to the hub properly, and could lead to warped discs.

08 Locate the new disc on the hub, then fit the retaining screw(s) and tighten securely. Bear in mind that the grooves should "face" the same way as the front discs.

09 The brake pad with the lug on its backing plate is the inner pad. Refit the anti-rattle springs to the pads, so that when the pads are fitted in the caliper, the spring end will be located at the opposite end of the pad, in relation to the pad retaining plate. Smear a little copper grease onto the back of the brake pads.

10 Slide the inner pad into position in the caliper, ensuring that the lug on its backing plate is aligned with the slot in the caliper piston.

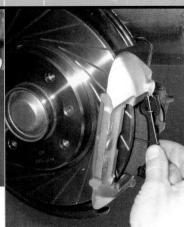

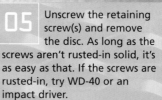

03 Using a pair of pliers, withdraw both the inner and outer pads from the caliper. Make a note of the correct fitted position of the anti-rattle springs, and remove the springs from each pad.

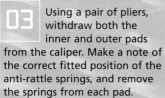

04 Make sure the caliper is clean, and free from dust and dirt - giving it a spray with some brake cleaner is a good move. Using a screwdriver in the notches provided, turn the caliper piston clockwise while pushing the piston back into its bore, until it is positioned like this. Watch the fluid level doesn't rise above the "MAXI" line in the master cylinder reservoir. If you're just changing your pads, go to Step 9).

05 Unscrew the retaining screw(s) and remove the disc. As long as the screws aren't rusted-in solid, it's as easy as that. If the screws are rusted-in, try WD-40 or an impact driver.

06 Ensure the new disc and the mating surface of the hub is perfectly clean. If the disc is covered with a preservative coating, degrease it thoroughly with brake cleaner.

Repeat the procedure on the opposite side. With both discs and pads correctly fitted, repeatedly press the brake pedal to force the pads onto the discs. Refit the wheels, then lower the car to the ground. Before driving the car, check the brake fluid level. Remember the discs and pads will need to "bed-in", so take it easy for the first hundred miles or so.

Locate the outer brake pad in the caliper body, ensuring that its friction material is **11** against the brake disc.

Ensure that the anti-rattle springs are correctly positioned, then slide the pad **12** retaining plate into place.

Fit a new spring clip into the hole in the pad **13** retaining plate (to stop it sliding out).

14

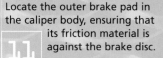

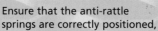

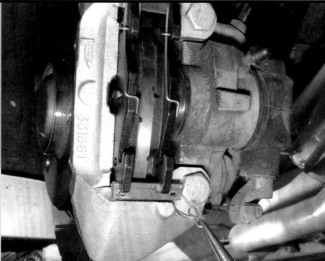

Interiors

As with most modern cars, the standard Saxo interior isn't particularly outstanding. Fear not, with a few modifications the overall look can be improved fairly easily and effectively. As with any cosmetic mod, beauty is in the eye of the beholder, so what you change and what sort of look you go for is very much up to you, but the interior really is one area where most of the goodies are pretty easy to fit.

Take one simply lovely standard interior...

Take it easy and break less

Many of the procedures we're going to show involve removing interior trim panels (either for colouring or to fit other stuff). Removal of interior panels can be tricky, and does require a bit of patience. Remember that most trim is only fragile plastic and is easily damaged, especially once it's had a chance to go a bit brittle with age.

Some panels will be secured with clips, which are available separately - when these break it's no real problem; just purchase new clips and fit them to the panel before refitting. However, more commonly the panel retaining clip or lug is actually an integral part of the panel. Breaking this type of clip is more of a problem; to renew the clip you've got to replace the panel. Don't replace the panel, and you're left with a panel which won't clip back into position, so it won't fit properly or will squeak annoyingly for the rest of its useful life.

If you come across a stubborn panel, before you reach for that crowbar, stop and check a few things:

• Make sure all the retaining screws and clips have been removed.
• Check that none of the surrounding panels need to be removed first. The surrounding panels can overlap the panel you are trying to remove, and maybe conceal a vital retaining clip or screw.
• Is the trim panel being retained by the door/tailgate sealing strip? If so, free the sealing strip from the body before trying to remove the panel.
• Are there any retaining screws still hidden behind trim caps?

When you're 100% sure all the fixings have been removed then, and only then, proceed to remove the panel. Remember that even with all the clips and screws removed, a surprising amount of force may still be needed to unclip the panel. It's just knowing when to use force, and how much. That's something which can't be explained but will come with experience. Just remember that a little extra time and care spent removing the panel can save you the cost and hassle of finding a replacement panel. The removal procedures for the more commonly-modded panels are covered, but we obviously haven't got space to cover the complete interior. That being said, with a bit of common sense and thought, the majority of panels can be removed fairly easily.

If you need more information, purchase our Saxo Service and Repair Manual (SRM 3506) which covers the interior (and rest of the vehicle) in detail.

...add some saucy kit, allow to simmer...

...and enjoy the tasty results.

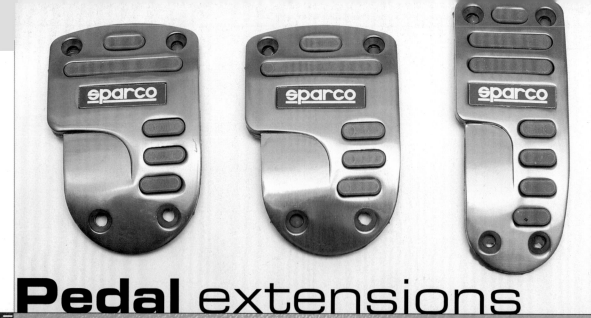

Pedal extensions

Pedal extensions are a simple item to fit, especially if you check a few things before purchasing them. The only problem which could crop up, is if the extension mounting points align with the pedal stems. Drilling holes through the pedals is easy, but not if the hole aligns with the pedal stem or its weld. Ideally, get yourself a set on which the mounting holes are positioned so they don't align with any of the pedal stems.

01 Prise off the old pedal rubbers. Offer the pedal extensions in, and establish exactly where they'll be mounted. Ensure that all three extensions can be correctly spaced, and that the mounting holes miss the pedal stem or its weld before going any further. If the mounting holes need altering, bear in mind that there's no way you'll be able to exchange them once you've taken a drill/file to them.

02 Hold the first extension firmly on its relevant pedal. Ensure the correct extension is positioned exactly as required, then scribe the required position of the mounting holes on the pedal.

03 Remove the pedal extension, and drill through one mounting holes in the pedal.

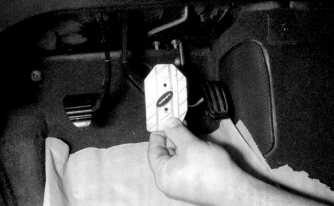

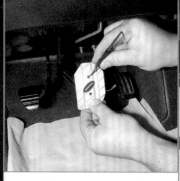

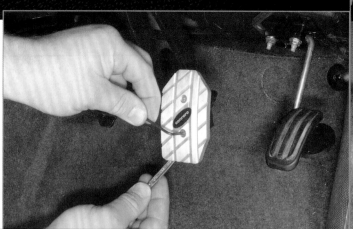

04 Fit one of the mounting bolts and secure the extension in position, tighten the mounting bolt nut lightly.

05 Align the extension correctly with the pedal then drill the second mounting hole in the pedal, using the extension as a template. This ensures the hole will align perfectly. (This is the correct way to do it, although we decided to scribe both holes first and then drill the holes.) Fit the second mounting bolt and nut, then securely tighten both mounting bolt nuts. Ensure the extension is securely fitted.

Tricks 'n' tips
The brake and clutch pedal extensions must be fitted with rubbers. If you fit pedal extensions without any sort of rubber to the brake and clutch pedals, your car will not pass an MOT test (it doesn't matter on the accelerator pedal).

Repeat the procedure on the remaining pedals until all three pedal extensions are correctly installed. When we fitted the clutch pedal extension, we found that we had to bend the pedal upwards slightly to enable us to fit the extension properly. **06**

When fitting the extension on the accelerator pedal, we found it easier to remove the pedal, as it conveniently unclips at the top, swings down, and then slides off to the side. When you're done, check that the pedals all still function correctly and **07**

don't catch on any surrounding components (like carpet, for instance). Remember - the new pedals will obviously feel different for a while, so take it a bit easy until you and your new pedals are working in perfect harmony.

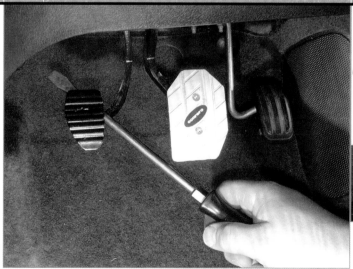

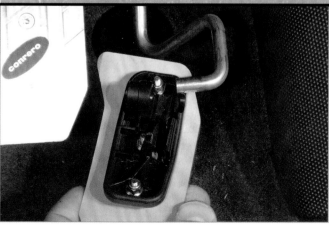

Sport
steering wheel

A new wheel is an essential purchase to enhance your interior. After all it's one of the main points of contact between you and the car, it's sat right in front of you, and the standard one is not pretty. When choosing your wheel remember that (like so much in life) size matters; the smaller the wheel, the more force you'll need to turn it. If you haven't got power steering, bear this in mind before purchasing the smallest wheel offered.

A trick feature which maybe worth investigating is the so-called "snap-off" wheel/boss. This feature comes in handy when you park up and would rather the car was still there when you come back. At present, the only company making removable wheels which are TUV-approved is Raid.

A word about airbags

Most Saxos have a driver's airbag fitted to the original wheel. So far, the market for replacement wheels with airbags is tiny, so fitting your tasty new wheel means losing what some people think is a valuable safety feature. Getting the airbag system disabled is one option - you'll have to ask a Citroën dealer if this is possible (the control unit is located under the centre console, and also operates the front seat belt tensioners).

But the problem with airbags doesn't end with simply disconnecting it, because all that'll happen then is your airbag warning light will be on permanently. Not only is this extremely irritating, it'll also be one of the reasons your newly-modded motor will fail the MOT (having the airbag itself isn't compulsory, but if the warning light's on, it's a fail - at least at the time this was written).

Two ways round this - either take out the clocks to deal with the offending warning light bulb, or bridge the airbag SRS connector plug pins (yellow plug, inside the steering wheel) with two lengths of wire attached to either side of a 5A fuse. Bridging the pins this way "fools" the test circuit (which fires up every time you switch on the ignition) into thinking the airbag's still there, and the warning light will go out as it should.

Warning: Airbags are expensive to replace (several £100s), and are classed as an explosive. For a safety item, there's any number of ways they can cause injuries or damage if you're not careful - check this lot out:

a) Before removing the airbag, the battery must be disconnected (don't whinge about it wiping out your stereo pre-sets). When the battery's off, don't start taking out the airbag for another 10 minutes or so. The airbag system stores an electrical charge - if you whip it out too quick, you might set it off, even with the battery disconnected.

b) When the airbag's out, it must always be stored the correct way up.

c) The airbag is sensitive to impact - dropping it from sufficient height might set it off. Even if dropping it doesn't actually set it off, it probably won't work again, anyway. By the way, once an airbag's gone off, it's scrap. You can't stuff it back inside.

d) If you intend to keep the airbag with a view to refitting it at some stage (like when you sell the car), store it in a cool place - but bear in mind that the storage area must be suitable, so that if the airbag went off by accident, it would not cause damage to anything or anyone. Sticking it under your bed might not be such a good idea.

e) If you're not keeping the airbag, it must be disposed of correctly (don't just put it out for the bin men). Contact your local authority for advice.

f) Airbags must not be subjected to temperatures in excess of 90°C (194°F). Just remember that bit about airbags being an explosive - you don't store dynamite in a furnace, now do you? Realistically in this country, the only time you'll get that hot is in a paint-drying oven.

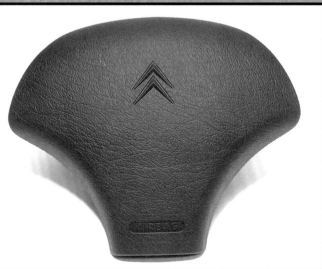

Fitting a **Momo** **wheel**

01 First set the front wheels to the straight-ahead position, and release the steering lock. Disconnect the battery negative lead, if it isn't already. Wait at least 10 minutes before you do anything else. This time allows the system capacitors to discharge, and should stop the airbag from accidentally going off.

02 Next, we need to move the centre console to one side to disconnect the airbag. Unclip the gear lever gaiter at the back, to reveal a Torx screw. Remove the screw …

Attention!
If you remove an airbag, you are disabling a safety-related system. Make sure you tell your insurance company.

07 Carefully lift the airbag out of the wheel, and disconnect the yellow SRS (supplemental restraint system, or airbag) connector.

08 Slacken and remove the wheel retaining bolt - Torx, size T50 on our car. Hold the wheel straight if you can, while you do this.

09 Pull the steering wheel off the column. If it's tight, refit the retaining bolt a few turns, to stop the wheel flying off, and tap it up near the centre using the palm of your hand or twist it back-and-forth whilst pulling upwards on it.

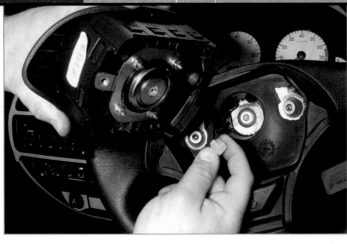

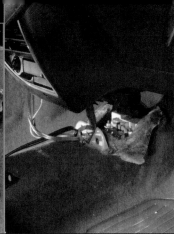

03 . . . and move the console to one side. Doing this provides us with more access to the SRS module, which appears, on the floor, as a big lump hidden underneath the carpet, behind the dashboard bracket.

04 Cut the carpet, and peel it apart to reveal the module.

05 Disconnect the multi-plug from the module. Wrap the plug up in insulating tape, so there's no risk of any of the terminals making contact. Cover up the module with the carpet and reinstall the centre console.

06 Remove the two Torx screws from the rear of the steering wheel.

10 Remove the two Torx screws . . .

11 . . . and remove the steering column upper and lower cowl panels.

12 Disconnect the SRS wiring and wrap the connector in insulating tape. Tuck the connector away.

13 Remove the three retaining screws from the contact unit, and take it out of the steering column.

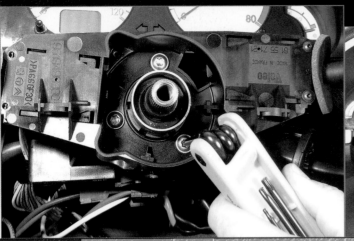

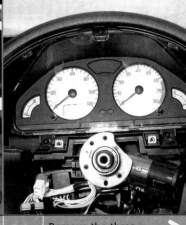

14 While you are here you may as well mask off the airbag warning light. This light will come on because we've disconnected the ECU. First, remove the three Torx screws which retain the steering column switches to the steering column.

15 Lift the switches towards you, and you'll now be able to access the lower two of the four instrument surround retaining screws (the other two are inside the surround, at the top). Remove the four screws and lift out the surround.

16 Remove the three instrument panel retaining screws (two at the bottom, one at the top) and lift out the instrument panel.

>

20 . . . and tape over the airbag warning light graphic. Refit the instrument panel back into the car.

21 Replace the steering cowling. Ensure the direction indicator switch is in the central ("off") position. If the steering wheel has got a self-cancelling lug and the indicator switch is not centrally positioned, the switch could be broken as the wheel is installed.

22 Put the steering boss into position taking note of the "TOP" marking.

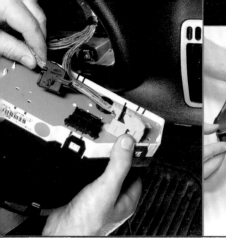

17 Unclip the multi-plugs from the back of the instrument panel.

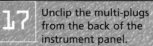

18 Carefully release the retaining lugs from around the instrument panel, and separate the dial section of the unit from the plastic viewer.

19 Lift off the warning lights illustration strip from the back of the plastic viewer . . .

. . . followed by the metal plate - this is actually the earth contact for the horn button, which you won't need.

23 Fit the boss gaiter . . .

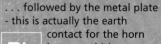

24

25 Put the steering wheel into position . . . >

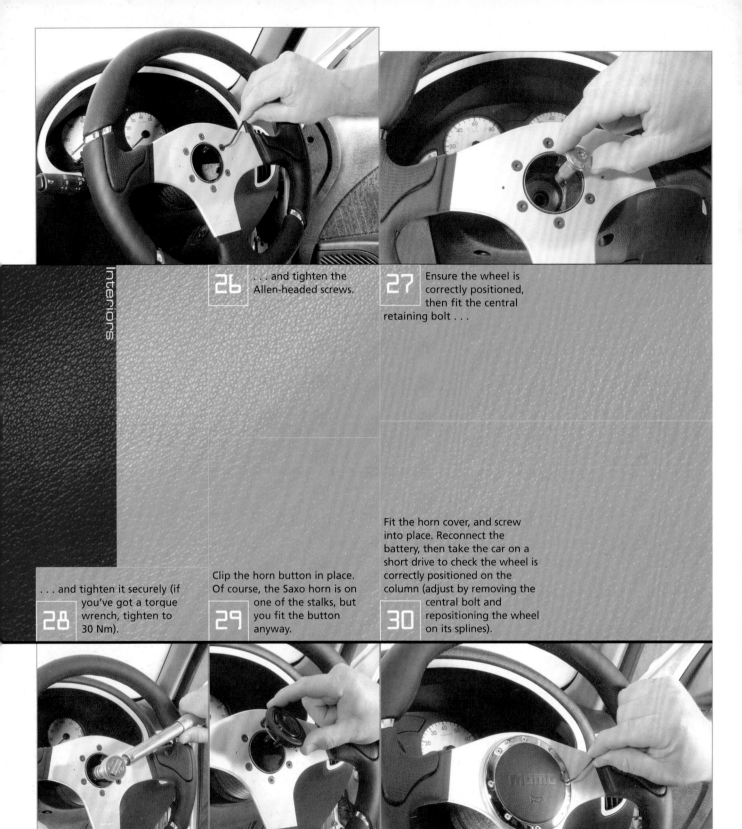

26 . . . and tighten the Allen-headed screws.

27 Ensure the wheel is correctly positioned, then fit the central retaining bolt . . .

Fit the horn cover, and screw into place. Reconnect the battery, then take the car on a short drive to check the wheel is correctly positioned on the column (adjust by removing the central bolt and repositioning the wheel on its splines).

28 . . . and tighten it securely (if you've got a torque wrench, tighten to 30 Nm).

29 Clip the horn button in place. Of course, the Saxo horn is on one of the stalks, but you fit the button anyway.

30

Tarting up your trim

The interior trim on the Saxo is pleasantly curvaceous, and doesn't rattle much. And that's the best we can say about it. Fortunately, there's plenty you can do to personalise it, and there are three main routes to take:

1) Adhesive or shrink-fit film - available in carbon, ally, and walnut (Don't!). Probably best used on flatter surfaces, or at least those without complex curves, or you'll have to cut and join - spray is arguably better here.

2) Spray paint - available in any colour you like, as long as it's… not black. This stuff actually dyes softer plastics and leather, and comes in a multi-stage treatment, to suit all plastic types. Special harder-wearing spray is required for use on steering wheels (but that's not really a good idea). Remember that ordinary spray won't "stick" too well to plastics (it might even damage some), won't be elastic, and will wear off.

3) Replacement panels - the easiest option, as the panels are supplied pre-cut, ready to fit. Of course, you're limited then to styling just the panels supplied.

If you fancy something more posh, how about trimming your interior bits in leather? Available in various colours, and hardly any dearer than film, you also get that slight "ruffled" effect on tighter curves.

Painting
interior trim

One thing to realise is that painting trim is a multi-stage application. You can't get away with just buying the top coat.

Even the proper interior spray top coat won't stay on for long without the matching primer, and the finish won't be wear-resistant without the finishing sealer spray. There's also a foaming cleaner you can buy, but you could get by with a general-purpose degreaser, such as meths. The only thing to watch is that the cloth doesn't turn too black when you're using your chosen solvent - if it does, you're damaging the finish. Providing you're a dab hand with the masking tape, paint gives you the flexibility to be more creative.

01 Clean up the surface to be sprayed, using a suitable degreaser. You must use something strong, to get off any silicone-based products you or the previous owner may have used, as these are death to paint adhesion. If you're not going to paint the whole thing, don't degrease the whole thing, or you might ruin the finish on the black bits.

02 Mask up the bits you don't want sprayed, as necessary. You can never do too much masking. Time taken masking will be repaid in time not spent re-doing the job.

03 Apply a mist coat of primer - this is essential to help the paint "stick" to the plastic. Allow plenty of time for the primer to dry.

04 Now for the topcoat - this should be applied very "dusty", which means you spray from slightly further away than normal, and let the paint fall onto the job, rather than blast it on using the full force of the aerosol spray. You may find that several coats are needed before it looks right - allow time for each one to dry (a few minutes) before banging some more on.

05 Once you've got even coverage, let the last top coat dry, then slap on the sealer coat. This doesn't give more shine, but improves wear-resistance. You should only need a light coat of sealer to finish the job. Let the paint go tacky (rather than fully dry) before peeling off the masking, and take care when you do - if the paint's too dry, you'll peel some of the paint off with the mask. If you're in any doubt, take your steadiest hand and a sharp knife to the edges of the masking tape before peeling.

Filming
your Saxo

If you fancy creating a look that's a bit more special than plain paint colours, film is the answer - but be warned - it's not the easiest stuff in the world to use, and so isn't everyone's favourite. If you want the brushed-aluminium look, or fancy giving your Saxo the carbon-fibre treatment, there really is no alternative (apart from the lazy-man option of new panels, of course).

01 First clean and degrease - see "Painting interior trim". On a heavily-grained finish (such as the glovebox lid), remember that the grain will show through the film - this does slightly ruin the effect, and a deep grain means the film won't stick all over the surface. It's not a good idea to rub stuff down with wet-and-dry, to get rid of the grain - you'll destroy the surface totally.

02 Cut the film roughly to size, remembering to leave plenty of excess for trimming - it's also a good idea to have plenty to fold around the edges, because the film has a nasty habit of peeling off, otherwise.

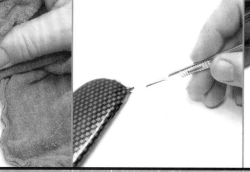

03 Stick the film on straight - very important with any patterned finish. Start at one edge or corner, and work across, to keep the air bubbles and creases to a minimum. If you get a really bad crease, it's best to unpeel a bit and try again - the adhesive's very tacky, and won't slide into position.

04 Work out the worst of the air bubbles with a soft cloth - get the stuff to stick as best you can before trimming, or it'll all go wrong. To be sure it's stuck (especially important on a grained surface), go over it firmly with the edge of a credit card type bit of plastic. Smooth around the edges with a soft cloth or rag, to make sure they're stuck.

05 Once the film's basically laid on, it's time for trimming - which as you've possibly guessed is the tricky bit. We found it was much easier to trim up the awkward bits once the film had been warmed up using a hairdryer or heat gun, but don't overdo it. Trim the edges - here, the corners are tricky, but by slitting the film, you can wrap the edges quite neatly. Make sure you've also got a very sharp knife - a blunt one will ripple the film, and may tear it.

06 On a tricky corner, heating the film helps it wrap round, and it keeps its shape - meaning it shouldn't try and spring back, ruining all your hard work. If you're still worried the edges will lift, the instructions suggest painting on some nail varnish. You could also use lacquer.

Ready-made panels

A far easier route is pre-finished panels. If you're determined that several panels are going to get "the treatment", don't be in too much of a hurry to take the easy option - mixing new panels with film is okay, but film with paint can look poor.

01 Clean the trim that you're going to apply the sticky stuff to thoroughly, with the cleaner supplied in the kit.

02 Heat the trim with a hairdryer or hot-air gun (don't melt it).

03 Heat the sticky stuff (again don't melt it).

04 Peel off the backing and stick to your trim. Using a cloth, rub over the newly-covered trim, to make sure the sticky stuff has stuck.

05 Heat the trim again, just to assist the adhesive process.

06 Our kit included sections for the dash centre section (with the radio/heater controls), the glovebox handle, and both dash end vents.

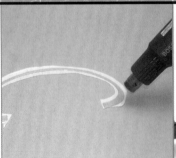

Citroën Saxo

Are you **sitting stylishly?**

The perfect complement to your lovingly-sorted interior is a set of race style seats. Besides the seat itself, remember to price up the subframe to adapt it to the mounting points in your car. Most people also choose the three- or four-point harnesses to go with it, but make sure the harness you buy is EC-approved, or an eagle-eyed MOT tester might make you take 'em out. Some seats are generally non-reclining, so it's important to try them out before you buy.

01 Remove the four seat retaining bolts - the inner front one's buried down next to the handbrake, but the outer one's more obvious.

02 The two rear bolts are pretty easy to spot, once the seat's slid forward. As you're taking the old seat out, disconnect the wiring plug under the seat -

this is for the seat belt tensioners (which, if you've disconnected the airbag when you fitted your sports steering wheel, don't work any more anyway).

03 Fit the new seat's subframe, and secure in place using the supplied washers and bolts.

>

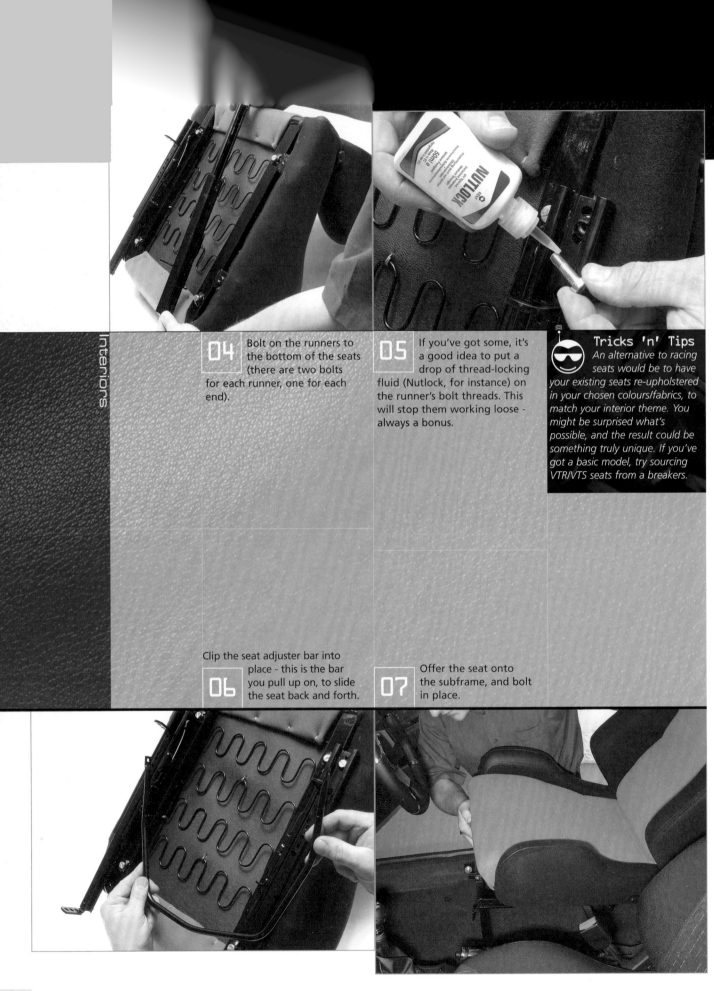

04 Bolt on the runners to the bottom of the seats (there are two bolts for each runner, one for each end).

05 If you've got some, it's a good idea to put a drop of thread-locking fluid (Nutlock, for instance) on the runner's bolt threads. This will stop them working loose - always a bonus.

Tricks 'n' Tips

An alternative to racing seats would be to have your existing seats re-upholstered in your chosen colours/fabrics, to match your interior theme. You might be surprised what's possible, and the result could be something truly unique. If you've got a basic model, try sourcing VTR/VTS seats from a breakers.

06 Clip the seat adjuster bar into place - this is the bar you pull up on, to slide the seat back and forth.

07 Offer the seat onto the subframe, and bolt in place.

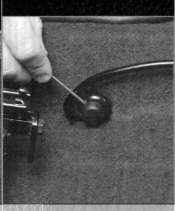

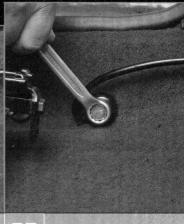

Race harnesses

The only problem with harnesses is caused by where you mount them. With all harnesses, you end up using one of the rear seat belt mounts, and it seriously reduces your ability to carry bodies in the back seats. The MOT crew say that, if you've got rear seats, you must have rear seat belts fitted, so you either "double-up" on your rear belt mounts (use the same mounts for your harnesses and rear belts) or you take the back seats out altogether. One thing you must never do is to try making up your own seat belt/harness mounting points. Citroën spent plenty of time selecting mounting points and testing them for strength. Drilling your own holes and sticking bolts through for belts is a no-no. We're not convinced either that the practice of slinging harnesses round a rear strut brace is wise, as some strut braces available are so flimsy you could bend it in a crash.

 01 Prise off the trim cap ...

02 ... and remove the lower anchorage bolt.

 Pull out the seat belt rail from its location. You might need to wiggle it. **03**

Prise off the cap and remove the upper mounting bolt. **04**

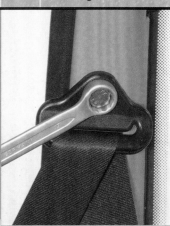

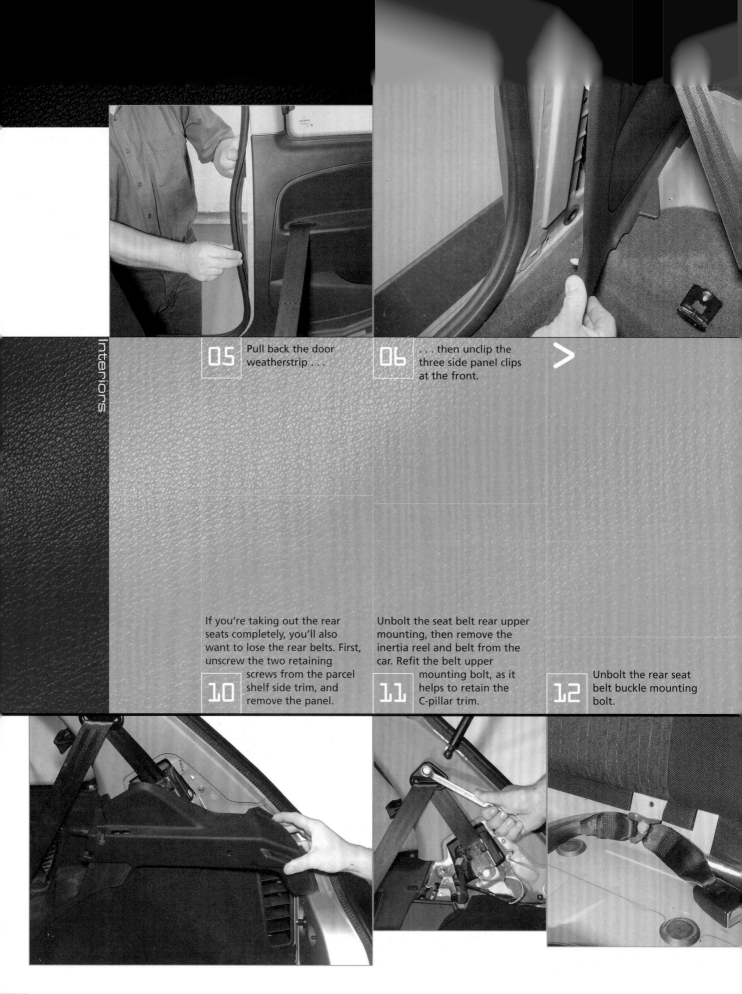

05 Pull back the door weatherstrip . . .

06 . . . then unclip the three side panel clips at the front.

>

If you're taking out the rear seats completely, you'll also want to lose the rear belts. First, unscrew the two retaining screws from the parcel shelf side trim, and remove the panel.

10

Unbolt the seat belt rear upper mounting, then remove the inertia reel and belt from the car. Refit the belt upper mounting bolt, as it helps to retain the C-pillar trim.

11

Unbolt the rear seat belt buckle mounting bolt.

12

  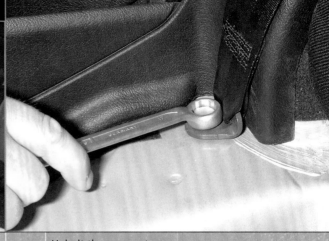

07 Prise out the plastic guide trim from the seat belt hole in the side trim panel.

08 At last we can see the seat belt inertia reel - remove the single mounting bolt, and remove the entire seat belt from the car.

09 Unbolt the rear seat belt lower mounting plate - you'll need to tilt up (or completely remove) the rear seat cushion for best access to this.

13 Thread the new belt through the seat, and secure the first harness mounting to the seat subframe (it's located down near the handbrake). Next, secure the second harness mounting to the lower anchorage point. It goes without saying that seat belt mounting bolts should be done up tight - 20 Nm, if you've got a torque wrench.

14 Bolt the third and fourth harness mountings to the two rear mountings, at the side and in the centre, and it's job done.

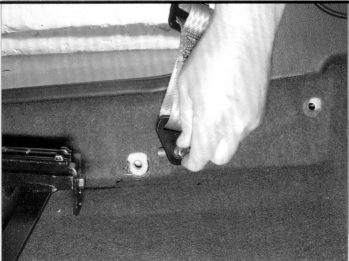 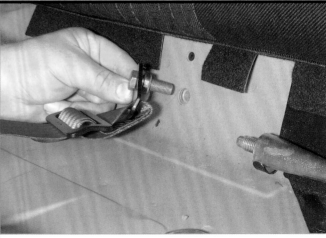

Boring flooring?

If you're thinking about removing the carpet remember that ripping out the old carpets is actually quite a major undertaking - first, the seats have to come out, and the carpets and underfelt fit right up under the dashboard, and under all the sill trims and centre console, etc. Carpet acts as sound-deadening, and is a useful thing to hide wiring under, too, so don't be in too great a hurry to ditch it completely.

A popular halfway-house measure to a fully decked-out chequerplate interior are the tailored footwell 'plates.Chequerplate is a popular material, and it's easy to see why it'll probably have an enduring appeal - it's tough but flexible, and easy to cut and shape to fit, and it matches perfectly with the racing theme so often seen in the modified world, and with the ally trim that's widely used too. In time, it will surely become available in a range of colours (the only one other than basic silver available is a rather nifty blue).

If you're completely replacing the carpet, do this at a late stage, after the ICE install and any other electrical work's been done - that way, all the wiring can be neatly hidden underneath it.

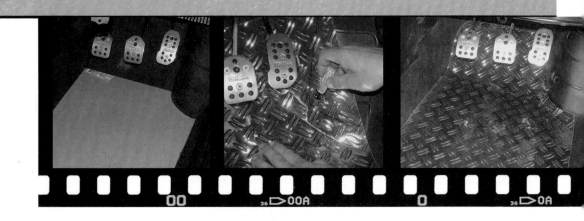

Changing
your knob

The choice out there is huge; fortunately, fitting's pretty easy, and even if your chosen knob is different to ours, the fitting details should be much the same.

01 First, unclip the gear lever gaiter.

02 The knob will need a mighty pull to remove it. But it will come off eventually.

03 Cut the gear knob off its rubber mounting, using a hacksaw blade. Save as much of the rubber mount as poss - you'll need it again.

04 Temporarily refit the rubber mounting to the gear lever . . .

05 . . . and carefully trim down the location lugs from the gear lever sleeve. These are what stopped you getting the old knob off, so don't feel you have to be gentle.

06 Now you need to cut off the pointy bit from the gear lever sleeve.

>

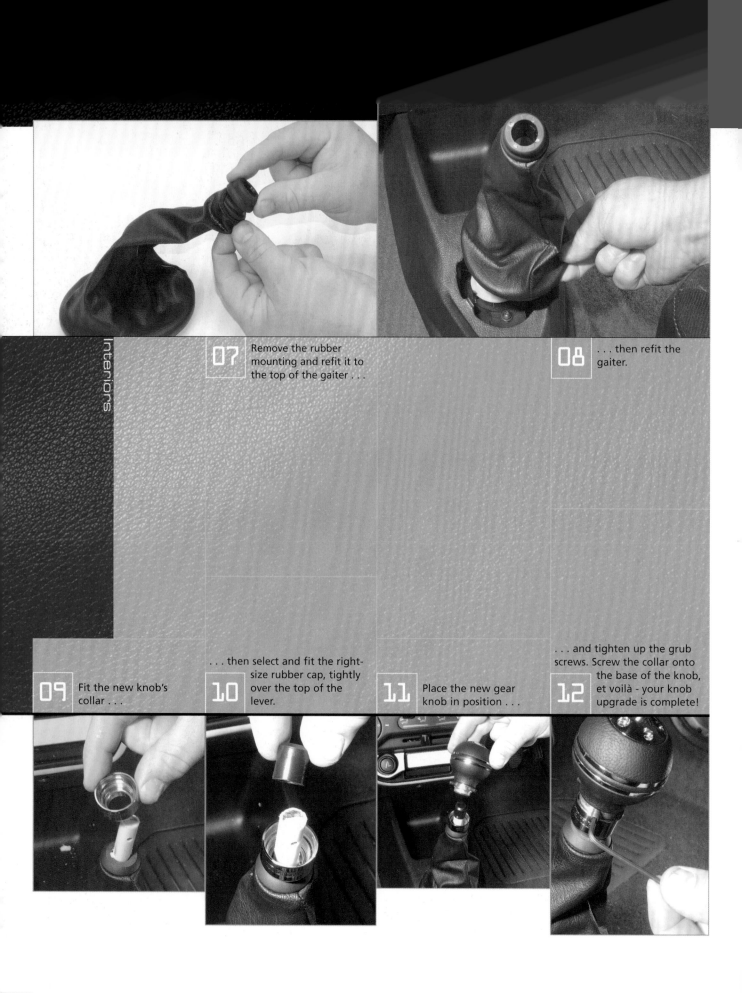

07 Remove the rubber mounting and refit it to the top of the gaiter . . .

08 . . . then refit the gaiter.

09 Fit the new knob's collar . . .

10 . . . then select and fit the right-size rubber cap, tightly over the top of the lever.

11 Place the new gear knob in position . . .

12 . . . and tighten up the grub screws. Screw the collar onto the base of the knob, et voilà - your knob upgrade is complete!

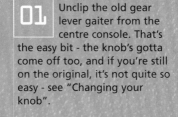

01 Unclip the old gear lever gaiter from the centre console. That's the easy bit - the knob's gotta come off too, and if you're still on the original, it's not quite so easy - see "Changing your knob".

Gear lever
gaiter & surround

Unclip and remove the white gear lever collar. We found that our sleeve trim wouldn't slip down over the lever, as the lever itself has a bend in it. Fortunately, removing the gear lever for straightening isn't hard at all.

02

Now get under the car and remove the heatshield from behind the exhaust pipe. It's held on by a few funny-looking nuts, which hopefully won't have rusted solid for you...

03

Unbolt the gear linkage. Just one nut and bolt, and no need to mark anything beforehand - simple.

04

>

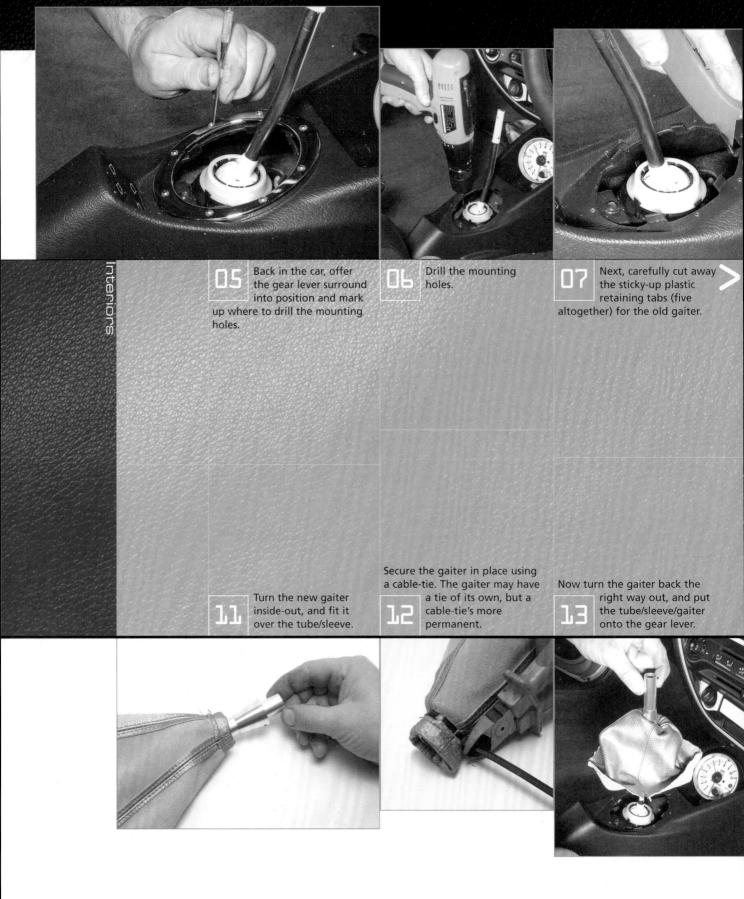

05 Back in the car, offer the gear lever surround into position and mark up where to drill the mounting holes.

06 Drill the mounting holes.

07 Next, carefully cut away the sticky-up plastic retaining tabs (five altogether) for the old gaiter. >

11 Turn the new gaiter inside-out, and fit it over the tube/sleeve.

12 Secure the gaiter in place using a cable-tie. The gaiter may have a tie of its own, but a cable-tie's more permanent.

13 Now turn the gaiter back the right way out, and put the tube/sleeve/gaiter onto the gear lever.

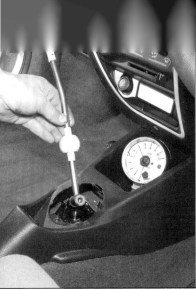

08 Lift the gear lever out of the car. It may need some persuading, because the ball joint has got to pass through a tight rubber gaiter.

09 You may have to trim some of the white plastic off the top of the gear lever, so's the gaiter sleeve and tube will pass over it. Once you've done that, it's off to the nearest vice for a spot of straightening. It doesn't have to be dead straight - just work it enough to let the sleeve slip over it. Refit your gear lever, connect the linkage and slide on the heatshield.

10 Fit the sleeve over the tube, and do up the grub screw.

Fit your new gear knob, and adjust the length of the tube/sleeve so that it fits neatly underneath your knob. Remember to leave some room at the bottom, so you don't have to **14** cut off too much of the gaiter. Secure in place with its grub screw.

Screw the surround into place, making sure that there's enough gaiter for gear lever movement, **15** but trapping the rest underneath the surround.

16 Finally, trim away the gaiter you don't want, and you're done.

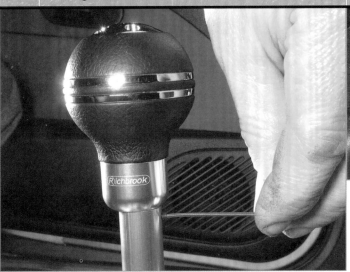

Handbrake
lever & gaiter

∧

01 Using a Stanley knife, carefully slice down and cut off the handbrake lever rubber . . .

02 . . . yes, really.

03 Our gaiter had Velcro round the base, for sticking to the carpet. Our mechanic wasn't convinced it would stick, so he tried it on his stubble. Hmm - that's attractive.

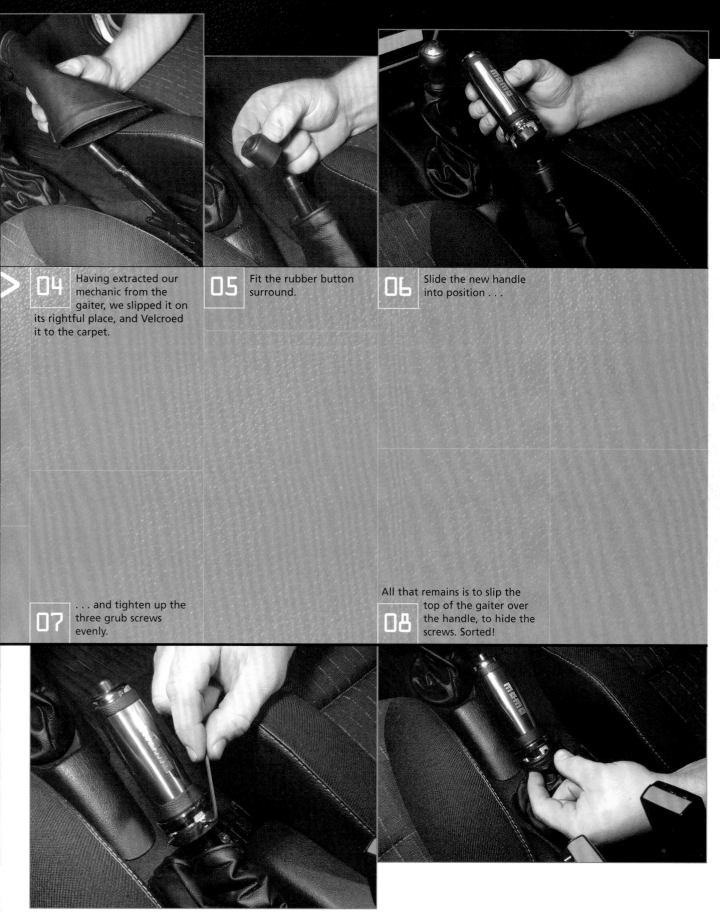

04 Having extracted our mechanic from the gaiter, we slipped it on its rightful place, and Velcroed it to the carpet.

05 Fit the rubber button surround.

06 Slide the new handle into position . . .

07 . . . and tighten up the three grub screws evenly.

08 All that remains is to slip the top of the gaiter over the handle, to hide the screws. Sorted!

Door trim panels

We removed our door trims for various reasons throughout the book, but the main reason was to get them re-trimmed, using the same colour and type material as our Corbeau seats (we ordered our material direct from Corbeau). Unfortunately, we don't have any pictures showing you how the panels were trimmed up, but it's worth sending them away, like we did, so the job gets done professionally. You get a better result, and there's someone else to blame if you're not happy. Most of the upholsterers in Yellow Pages should be able to tackle the job, but it's better still if they've got car experience - our chosen pros certainly have.

01 Unclip and remove the triangular panel containing the adjustable knob for the door mirror.

02 Remove the Torx screw and release the mirror knob.

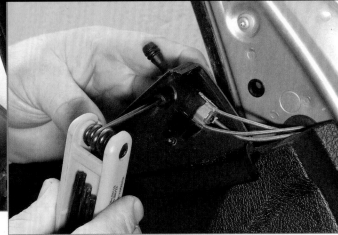

> **03** Unclip the speaker grille.

04 Remove the Torx screw at the front of the door panel . . .

05 . . . and the one inside the door pull, which then lifts out. If you've got wind-up windows, also pull off the window winder handle.

06 Unclip the door panel from the door, and carefully pull the panel away from the door - the door handle should unclip itself.

07 As you can see, our newly-trimmed-up door looks really smart.

Remote tailgate release
using rear wiper switch

What you need is a solenoid kit, which consists of a solenoid, fuse, electrical wiring, overload switch, cable and dashboard switch. Now there are two ways of doing this - you can either use your rear wiper switch to open the boot (that's only if you've removed your rear wiper), or you can install the switch provided. We did both so that you have a choice.

01 Open the tailgate. Remove the three screws (one at each side, one in the pull handle) securing the trim panel, release the securing clips and remove the panel.

02 Cut out a piece of metal plate and mount it to the tailgate with some self-tapping screws - this is to give you a mounting plate for the new solenoid.

03 Offer up the solenoid and bracket so that the solenoid's operating cable is aligned with the tailgate lock lever.

04 Mark the metal plate so you know where to mount the solenoid bracket . . .

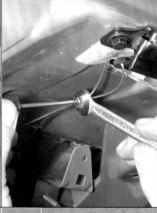

> 05 . . . then drill two holes in the plate, and fix the solenoid bracket to it.

06 Now refit the plate/bracket back onto the tailgate.

07 Clamp the solenoid to the bracket by tightening the retaining nuts and bolts.

08 Loop the cable through the tailgate lock lever and adjust the tension by feeding the cable through the clamp and tightening the clamp. Leave a little slack in the cable.

11 You need to trace three wires: Rear wiper wire (labelled 520), Rear washer wire (labelled 530), Earth wire (labelled M0005). Cut the rear wiper wire (520) and tape up the end leading to the wiper switch - you don't need this anymore. Now cut the rear WASHER wire (530), and join the switch end to the other end of the rear WIPER wire, which leads to the tailgate. Join the remaining washer wire (530, which leads to the washer pump) to the earth wire (M0005, a general wiring harness earth wire). See the diagram, it may help. That's it. When you try it out, if the solenoid pushes outwards and not inwards, swap the wires on the back of the solenoid.

Cut the wire (labelled 520) from the multi-plug that used to be fitted to your rear wiper motor. Crimp on a new terminal connector to it, and attach the wire to the remaining terminal on the solenoid. Refit the tailgate trim panel, and move yourself into the driver's footwell area. Remove the steering column cowl panels by removing the two Torx screws

Connect the earth wire to the solenoid and attach the other end to one of the metal plate mounting screws. Hide the overload switch in the tailgate aperture.

09

10 (see the steering wheel section if you're unsure)

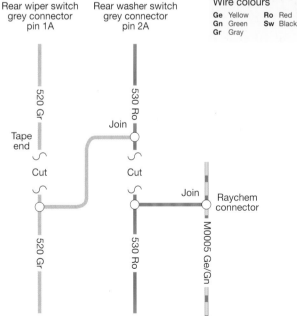

Rear wiper switch grey connector pin 1A

Rear washer switch grey connector pin 2A

Wire colours
Ge Yellow **Ro** Red
Gn Green **Sw** Black
Gr Gray

520 Gr

530 Ro

Join

Tape end

Cut

Cut

Join

Raychem connector

520 Gr

530 Ro

M0005 Ge/Gn

Rear wiper brown connector pin 1

Washer pump green connector pin 2

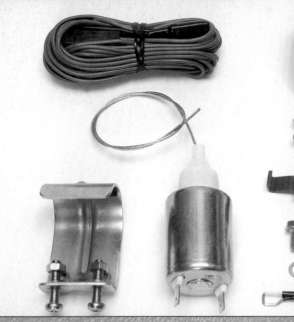

Remote tailgate release

using new switch (easier option)

01 Follow the procedure for using the rear wiper switch (though obviously you will have to mount the solenoid in a slightly different place, because your wiper motor will still be there). Follow the previous procedure up to the end of Step 9. Now connect the kit's red wire, which has an inline fuse, to a live terminal within the fusebox. Run the red wire through the bulkhead and into the driver's-side footwell.

Feed the wire up through the tailgate rubber boot, and into the tailgate. Connect the wire to the solenoid. When you try it out, if the solenoid pushes outwards and not inwards, swap the wires on the back of the solenoid.

02 Fabricate a bracket to mount the tailgate release switch.

03 Mount the switch to the driver's-side kick panel, and connect the red wire to the rear of the switch.

04 Connect the supplied green wire to the switch, and run the wire to the rear of the car.

05

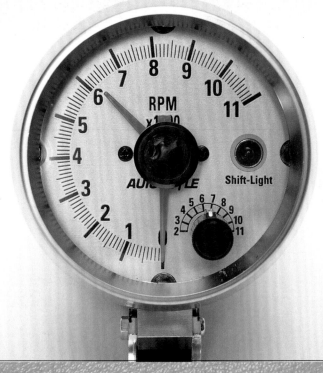

01 Check the back of the rev counter, and set the switch with regards to how many cylinders your car has.

02 Next, decide where you're going to stick it. Somewhere in clear view seems a good idea - so we decided to mount it in the centre console . . .

Fitting a
rev counter

Another racing touch is a rev counter with a "change-up" shift light. All you need now is the paddle gearchange! Some Saxos, of course, aren't graced with a rev counter, so here's how you can fit one.

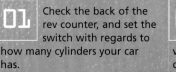

. . . but perhaps somewhere on the A-pillar trim or instrument pod would've been **03** better from a safety viewpoint?

04 Remove the centre console by unclipping the gear lever gaiter . . .

05 . . . removing the Torx retaining screw . . .

. . . and if applicable, disconnect the electric windows multi-plugs. Remove the **06** centre console from the car.

>

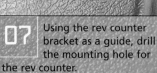

07 Using the rev counter bracket as a guide, drill the mounting hole for the rev counter.

08 Secure the rev counter bracket in place with the use of two screws and speed clips.

09 Now drill an additional hole for the wiring to go through. Fit the rev counter to its bracket, and feed the wiring through the hole.

10 Now you should have four wires coming from the back of the rev counter. The first one to fit is the earth, which can go to any convenient earth point. Remember where the airbag ECU is, from the steering wheel-fitting section? We attached our earth wire to the mounting screw of the airbag ECU.

11 On our Saxo, we took the green wire from the rev counter (signal wire) and spliced into the grey signal wire from the back of the diagnostic socket, near the fusebox. If you intend doing this job, it's a good idea to see if you can get hold of a wiring diagram for your model year.

12 Take the white wire from the rev counter, and splice it into the brown illumination wire from the back of the cigarette lighter.

13 Finally, you need to splice the last (red) rev counter wire into a positive (live) feed wire from the ignition switch. Now put everything back together, and you have now fitted your rev counter.

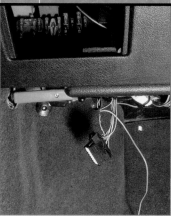

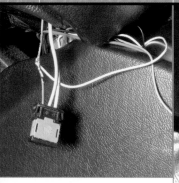

Push button start

Like to have a race-style starter button on your Saxo? Read on! A very cool piece of kit, and not too bad a job to wire up. The idea of the racing starter button is that the ignition key is made redundant, beyond switching on the ignition lights (it'd be a pretty negative security feature, if you could start the engine without the key at all).

This is one job where you'll be messing with big wires, carrying serious current - more than any other electrical job, don't try and rush it, and don't skimp on the insulating tape. Do it properly, as we're about to show you, and there's no worries. Otherwise, at best, you'll be stranded - at worst, there could be a fire.

01 The instructions here should be good for most makes. First, DISCONNECT THE BATTERY. You may have ignored this advice before. Don't do so now.

02 Remove the four blank switches from the centre dashboard panel - these just prise out.

Drill a hole in the plastic big enough for the switch to be mounted. The hole must line up with one of the gaps in the dashboard where you removed a blanking plug (not right in the middle of the plastic strip). Use the hole for one of the two middle blanking plugs, as the outer two will be used to mount the plastic strip. You'll see what we mean in a minute.

Get a piece of plastic, and cut it to size so that it is the length and width of the hole that the four blank switches came from. Black plastic is best, if you can get it, otherwise you'll have to spray or cover it later.

03

Using a Stanley knife, carefully cut the tops off two of the switch blanks, and they should end up like this.

04

05

>

06 Try the switch in the hole (don't fit it yet). Sand the plastic down to remove the rough edges, and spray it black or cover it, if you need to.

07 Fit the two modified blanking plugs back into the dashboard (one at either end, so that you are left with two holes in the middle). Glue the piece of plastic to the blanking plugs.

11 Next, splice into the vehicle ignition wire ("CC01" printed on it) and join the white wire from the new relay/fuse that you have fitted into it.

Wire colours		Key to items	
Ws	White	1	Battery
Br	Brown	2	Ignition switch
Bl	Blue	3	Engine fuse box
Sw	Black	4	Starter motor
		5	Line fuse
		6	Starter button relay
		7	Starter button

12 Now run the black wire from the new relay up behind the dashboard to the new starter button. Have a good look at the basic wiring diagram we've done for you. It should help.

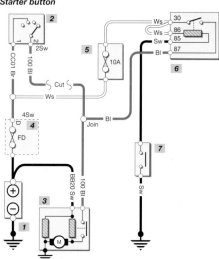

Starter button

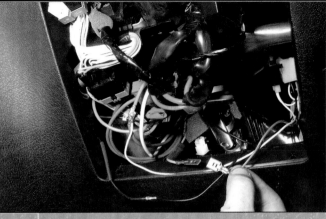

08 Just to give you an idea of what we're trying to do, here's the finished article removed. The switch fits into the plastic strip, with the two cut-down switch blanks glued on either end, to give support, and to locate it in the dash. Now it all makes sense!

09 While the glue's drying, remove the steering column shrouds, which are held together by two Torx screws Mount the fuse holder and relay just inside the facia using a self-tapping screw. The fuse must be mounted somewhere easy to get at, in case it blows.

10 Now to wire it up. Locate the ignition multi-plug (just down from the ignition switch) and disconnect the starter solenoid wire from the multi-plug (the wire has "100" printed on it). Connect the starter solenoid wire (100) to the blue wire which leads to the new relay you have just installed. Make sure that it is the starter solenoid wire you've connected, and not the (100) wire which goes to the ignition switch.

You then need to run an earth wire, from any convenient good earth, up to the new starter button. We used one of the **13** airbag ECU's mounting screws to trap our earth wire under.

Attach the wires to the back of the starter button, fit the button into the dashboard, and **14** test (after reconnecting the battery).

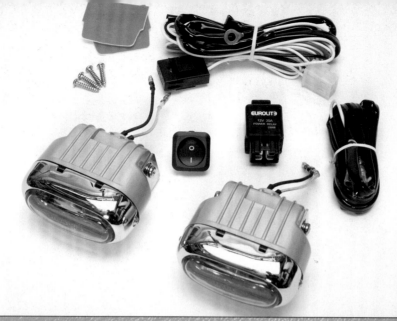

Fitting **showlights**

In-car lights are good to fit, to highlight all your tasteful mods at the cruise or show. If you've fitted a cage or other cool mods, it's only natural you'd want to show it all off. One word of caution - Mr Plod probably won't take kindly to these lights being on while you're driving at night, so fitting an easily-reached switch would be a good plan. We show you how.

01 First up, we're going to mount the new light switch. This is very similar to the remote starter button we fitted earlier (see "Push button start", and follow Steps 2 to 8). Here's our new switch mounted in the plastic strip described, minus the two end blanks.

02 While the glue's drying on your switch panel, go to the boot and remove the parcel shelf side trim panels (2x Torx screws).

03 You may still have the rear seat belts. If you do, remove the rear upper seat belt mounting bolt, and get the belt out of the way.

04 Offer up the lights, and mark where you want them fitted - in our case, it's on the C-pillar trim.

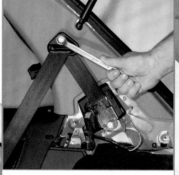

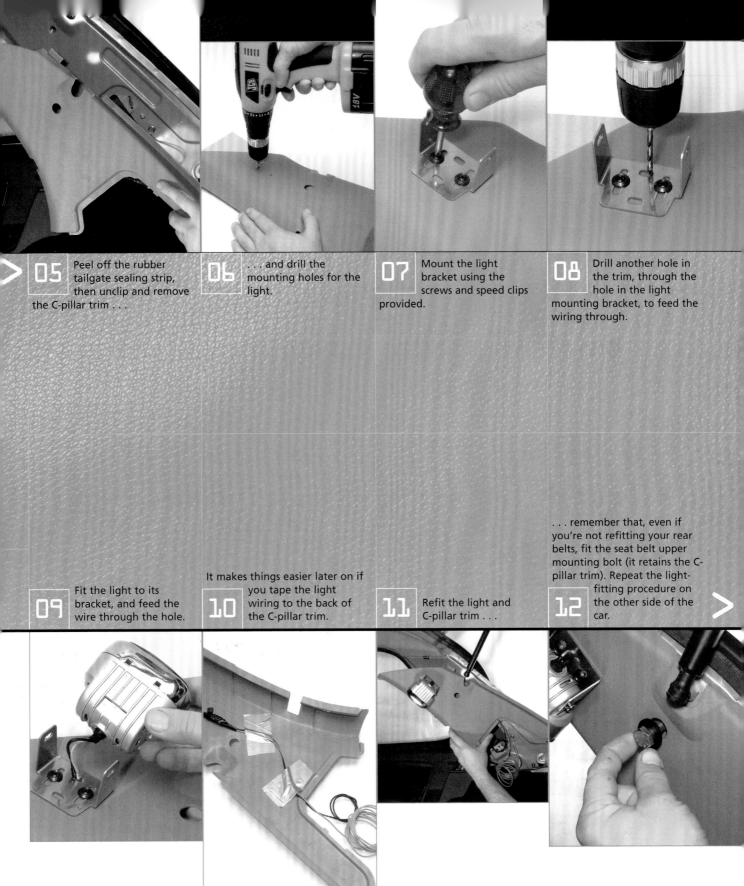

05 Peel off the rubber tailgate sealing strip, then unclip and remove the C-pillar trim . . .

06 . . . and drill the mounting holes for the light.

07 Mount the light bracket using the screws and speed clips provided.

08 Drill another hole in the trim, through the hole in the light mounting bracket, to feed the wiring through.

09 Fit the light to its bracket, and feed the wire through the hole.

10 It makes things easier later on if you tape the light wiring to the back of the C-pillar trim.

11 Refit the light and C-pillar trim . . .

12 . . . remember that, even if you're not refitting your rear belts, fit the seat belt upper mounting bolt (it retains the C-pillar trim). Repeat the light-fitting procedure on the other side of the car.

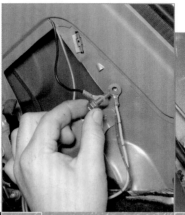

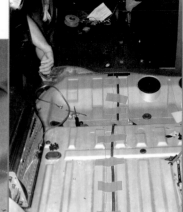

13 Earth each lamp to its own C-pillar, using the earthing point which is already there.

14 Run the wiring of each lamp into the boot and join the two wires together, using a junction connector, so that only one wire needs to run to the front of the car.

15 Run the wire up the car, through the bulkhead to around the fusebox area. Of course, you don't have to do it quite like we did.

16 Mount the supplied fuse and relay in the engine bay (make sure you remove the fuse first). Connect the relay terminal 85 to earth, then obtain a live feed from the fusebox, which runs through the new fuse and into the relay terminal 30. Attach the wire for the lights (which you've run through from the lights in the boot) to terminal 87 on the relay.

17 Tap into the live feed between the fuse and the relay, and run the wire back to the switch in the back of the dashboard. Also run a wire from the switch to the relay, and connect it to relay terminal 86.

18 Connect the two wires to the back of the switch, and fit the switch into the plastic plate. Refit the fuse under the bonnet, and try out your new showlights.

19 The finished switch should look something like this.

Interior show lights

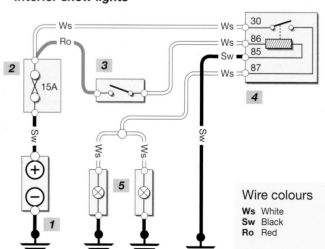

Wire colours

Ws White
Sw Black
Ro Red

Key to items

1 Battery
2 Line fuse
3 Show light switch
4 Show light relay
5 Show lights

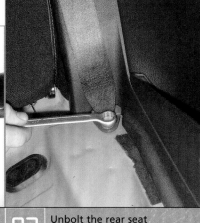

Fitting a
Show cage

A rollcage looks great especially when combined with sports seats and harnesses. Like the strut brace, a rollcage stiffens up the body, as well as providing strengthening should you end up on your roof. Er - well probably not in the case of a show cage, but it still looks great. However, the advantage of the show cage is that it's much easier to fit (and remove) than the real thing.

Unfortunately most insurance companies do not like rollcages. Definitely one to check before fitting.

01 Lift out your rear seat cushion and remove it from the car. Assemble the basic cage, as in top bar, the two side frames and the two corner pieces. Tighten the corner pieces in place by doing up their two screws, but do not tighten them too much - there must be a bit of movement available for now.

02 Unbolt the rear seat belt lower mounting.

03 Place the cage bracket over the seat belt mounting hole and refit the seat belt. Do the same on the other side.

04 Insert the whole cage frame into the car, and secure it to the cage brackets.

05 Unbolt the front seat belt upper mounting, and align the cage bracket over the hole. Insert a spacer between the seat belt mounting hole and the cage bracket.

06 Refit the front seat belt. If you are fitting (or have fitted) a four-point harness, use the bolt from the original front seat belts to secure the cage. Completely tighten the corner pieces of the cage.

Panelling rear
seat back rest

How's your woodworking skills? If you've ditched the rear seats, it could all be looking a bit bare in there. There are of course, plenty of options for all the resulting space - you could fill it with amps and subs, tastefully displayed on chequerplate, wild-coloured carpet or even leather. Trouble is, you need something to mount all these grand ideas on, to start with. A little bit of carpentry, a sheet or two of MDF, and you'll have a "canvas" to start "painting" your dream Saxo install on.

You'll need a large piece of cardboard, the size of your rear seat backrest. Remove the fabric panel from the rear of the backrest, to start with.

01

Measure the height of the backrest, mark it on the cardboard and cut the cardboard to size.

02

Pulling the foam to one side, draw around the metal of the backrest, to give the exact shape.

03

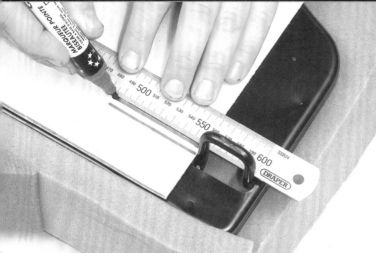

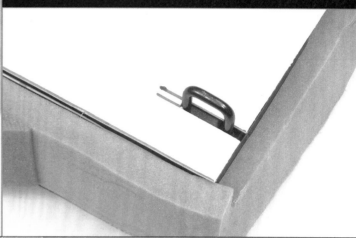

 04 Mark on the card the position of the backrest catch . . .

05 . . . then cut out the slot for the catch, and try it in place.

Attention!
MDF dust is nasty stuff to breathe in. Wear a mask when you're cutting, drilling or sanding it.

 06 Now using the card as a template, transfer the backrest shape onto the MDF.

07 Using a jigsaw, cut out the shape from the MDF. >

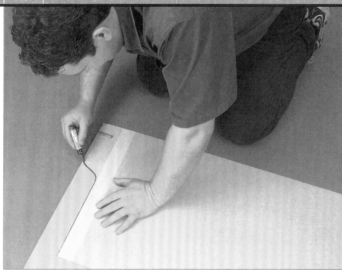

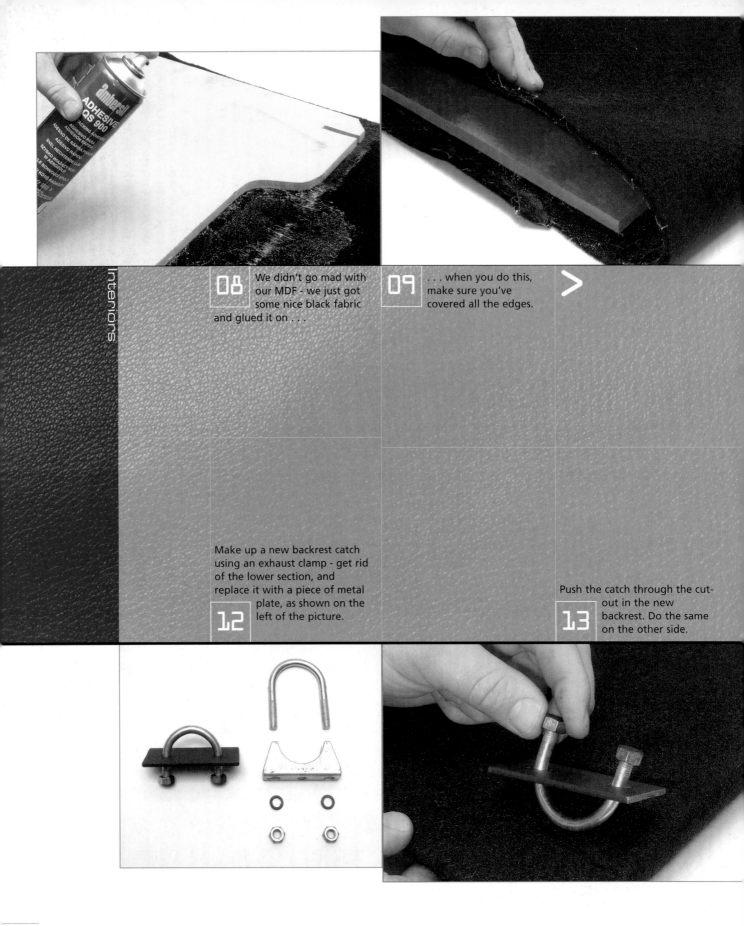

08 We didn't go mad with our MDF - we just got some nice black fabric and glued it on . . .

09 . . . when you do this, make sure you've covered all the edges.

>

12 Make up a new backrest catch using an exhaust clamp - get rid of the lower section, and replace it with a piece of metal plate, as shown on the left of the picture.

13 Push the catch through the cut-out in the new backrest. Do the same on the other side.

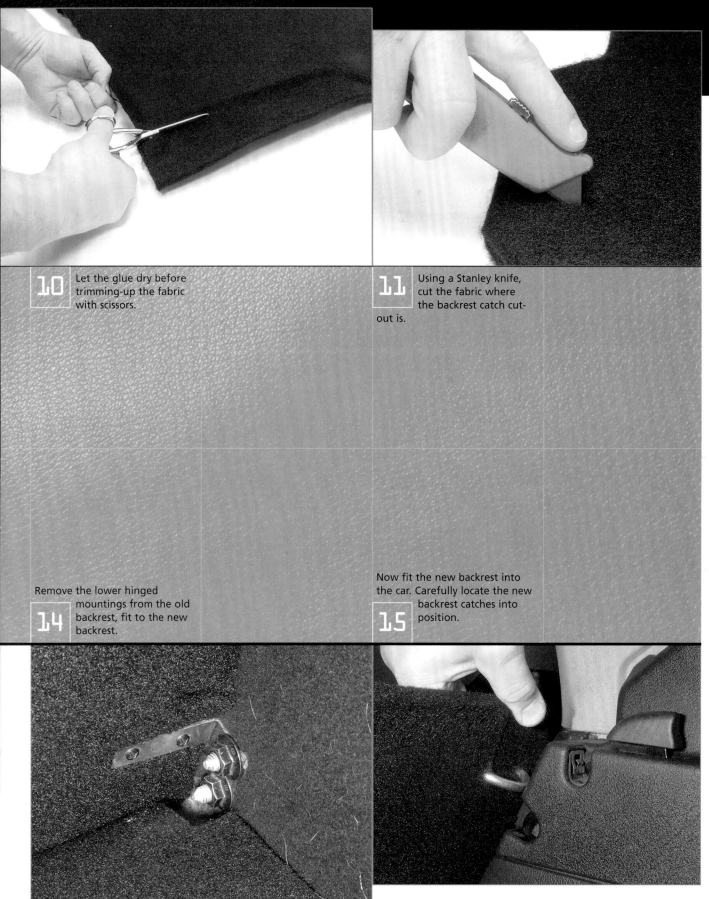

10 Let the glue dry before trimming-up the fabric with scissors.

11 Using a Stanley knife, cut the fabric where the backrest catch cut-out is.

14 Remove the lower hinged mountings from the old backrest, fit to the new backrest.

15 Now fit the new backrest into the car. Carefully locate the new backrest catches into position.

Panelling rear seat base

Rather than just leaving holes for your harnesses to poke through, how about getting some letterboxes with the bristle-type draught excluder strips, and putting them to better use? Nailed on underneath with self-tappers, it makes a nice finishing touch.

To mount the panel, buy some metal bracket strips from your local DIY or car accessory shop. Modify two strips to look like the bracket shown in our picture. Cut a hole in the carpet, and pass the bracket down so it fits over the rear seat mountings. Secure in place with a nut. Repeat at the other end of the seat. Fit the MDF in place, making sure it fits snug under the backrest section.

01 This procedure is much the same as the rear backrest, apart from the fact that you can't draw round the seat. Instead, you get your cardboard and mark it up while in the car, and cut out bits of card until it fits in all the nooks and crannies. One difference is that you have to mark up holes so that your seat belt harness will pass through it. Transfer the card template onto the MDF.

02 Cut out your MDF panel using a jigsaw, then glue it up and cover it in your chosen material.

03 finishing touch.

04 Secure the MDF in onto the new brackets with self-tapping screws.

05 One possible flaw in the plan is that longer seat belt bolts might be needed, to re-mount the harnesses. We had to make up and fit a spacer between the seat belt mounting point and the harness . . .

06 . . . to refit our harnesses properly. Fitting longer bolts and spacers should be okay, MOT-wise, as long as you don't try to bodge it. Remember that using any old bolt probably won't work - seat belt bolts have a fine-pitched thread, so don't try forcing anything else to fit. Check for a specialist nut 'n' bolt man in your Yellow Pages, and do it right.

Tax
disc
holder

Clean your window, and insert you tax disc into the holder. Stick the sticky pads onto the front of the holder.

Stick the holder to your window. Er... that's it. Our holder has a removable back, so you don't have to buy a new one for next year (or in 6 months' time). Nice touch.

Door lock
pins

First remove the door trim (as described in the relevant section). The pin itself is glued into position, and is difficult to get off. Using a hacksaw carefully cut away the plastic pin.

01

02 Put a bit of glue inside the new pin and screw it on. Err... that's it!

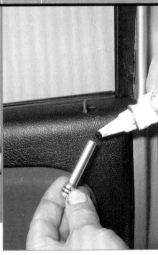

ICE

Head unit

To give your audio system a decent start, you need a good head unit to provide the signal that the amp will beef up, and that the speakers will replay. Now we know this probably looks a bit mental, but we weren't just swapping a CD player for a radio-cassette. We also added a CD autochanger that we hid away in the glovebox.

The only thing we noted of any difficulty was getting the head unit into place with its larger bundle of wiring. Eventually we got it in, but it did mean a lot of scratched hands and jiggling of wires until the unit finally slipped home.

Getting the Saxo's head unit out wasn't too difficult, it just needed a modified DIN removal key. These keys are the bent metal prongs that seem to get most original-fit radios out. We cut one in half, and inserted a prong into each side hole, and the player pulled straight out.

01

With the set hanging out you can see the connections on the back of it. The Saxo uses ISO plugs, which are pretty much an industry standard thing now. The Sony head unit we're using has all the necessary adaptors to couple up to these, so wiring it in is another simple job. You can also see the support bung on the back of the set that fits into a bracket in the dash and stops the unit bouncing up and down in the hole.

02

Once the old unit and its mounting sleeve had been removed, the Sony sleeve could be fitted, which just meant sliding it into the dash aperture. We then used a modified screwdriver to bend over the locating tags to hold the sleeve firmly in place.

03

Here the Sony wiring loom is being hooked up to complete the head unit's connections. You can also see the two phono leads that send signal to the amplifier, and the Unilink cable that goes to the CD player which we're putting into the glovebox.

04

05 This is the finished head unit wiring, and you can see that the new rear support has been added to the Sony. Now all we have to do is get it into the hole.

06 On the Saxo, getting the unit itself to slide home in the dash can be a bit of a pig to do as the aperture is a bit tight for space behind the unit. Do not force the unit in or you'll damage something. Keep gently moving the unit back and forward until the wiring loom shifts into the right place for the unit to pop into place with a click. Once it had clicked in, we added the trim surround to finish it off. Nice.

07 Here's the Sony CD autochanger, which was a dead easy fit in the glovebox. All we had to do was cut a little out of the side of the glovebox liner, and then make a surround to take up the gap around the front of it. Once that was covered with matching carpet and slipped over the changer, you get the result you see here. Very tidy, don't you think?

Amplifier

A decent car stereo system needs separate amplification. You'll be amazed at how much better a dedicated power amp is than a head unit alone.

For the Saxo we chose a Caliber four-channel amp, running the front speakers off two channels, and bridging up the other two to run the Dragster sub woofer. We left the head unit to drive the back shelf speakers.

01 The first job was to make a cardboard template to give the size and shape of the amp rack. The Saxo boot's not bad to add bits to, but we went for a simple flat rack on the passenger side to keep things usable.

Once the rack was bolted in place, using the bracket at the front and a single screw at the rear, the amp was attached and then wired up. The wires were terminated with crimped-on gold terminals, and these were neatened up with heatshrink tubing. This also colour-coded the wires - red for positive, black for negative - to aid correct connections. If you look at the bottom bolt you can just make out that the earth cable has been attached there to give a decent earth point for the system.

02 After cutting the template to the appropriate shape, the outline was transferred to MDF and then cut out. A bit of trial fitting and shaping was necessary to get the rack to sit properly against the boot side, and three strips of MDF were added to space it away from the boot sidewall, giving enough clearance to run the wiring behind the board.

The finished boot with the sub box and rear shelf in place shows the neat Neutrik plug that allows quick removal of the shelf. Remember to screw and bolt everything down for safety, and to stop things getting damaged by them rolling around the boot during 'spirited' driving.

The Caliber amp's pretty big so we laid it out to carefully plan the holes needed for the wiring and the fixing screws. Doing this meant the wires would just pop out from behind the panel and look nice and neat, and they'd be out of danger from stuff rolling round the boot. The holes were opened out with a cone drill to give enough room to route the cabling through. **03**

From this side you can see the spacer bars arranged around the rack, and you can see the bracket that will hold the front end of the rack in place. It bolts down under the rear seat hinge assembly, meaning there's no need to drill the car's bodywork. The rack was covered with black trunk-liner carpet to make it less visible, and to match the sub box. **04**

Front
speakers

Citroën's idea of front speakers left us feeling a bit flat. They were really poor, and not fit to go on the end of a decent system like this. There was only one thing for it, we were going to have to fit something worth listening to. We got hold of a set of JBL component speakers which are made up of a five-inch mid-range, a separate tweeter and a passive crossover. This splits the signal from the amp into treble for the tweeter, and everything else for the mid.

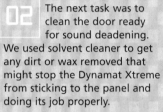

01 Removing the door panel was dead easy. Two Torx screws held it on through the front upper corner and down through the handle, and then it unclipped from the door. You can just un-clip the speaker grille from the panel if you like, but when you're doing a proper job, you need the panel out of the way. We found that the speakers were riveted in place, so the rivets had to be drilled out before the speakers could be removed.

02 The next task was to clean the door ready for sound deadening. We used solvent cleaner to get any dirt or wax removed that might stop the Dynamat Xtreme from sticking to the panel and doing its job properly.

While this new Dynamat doesn't need heating up like other sound deadening materials, it does need a good rolling to get the proper bond. We used a hardwood wallpaper edge roller to really get stuck in, making **03** sure the material went into every crease on the door.

Next we drilled out a small hole to allow the wiring to come through from the inside of the door. This was to allow us to lengthen the original wire that came into the door so that it **04** would reach to the intended position of the JBL crossover.

It also meant we could feed a wire back into the door cavity from the crossover to the mid-range speaker. To stop the new wire hole going rusty, we painted the bare edge and let it dry before we fitted a grommet to **05** protect the wires that would be fed through the door skin.

>

Next we cut off the speaker plug in the door, and stripped the insulation back, ready for soldering. **06**

> **07** We then joined new wire to the existing Saxo cabling, and covered the joints with heatshrink tubing to keep them safe.

08 Having pulled the extended wire through the grommet, we fed another piece back for the mid-range speaker and then fitted a terminal to it. Again we used heatshrink tubing to cover the new terminals and stop any possible shorting out.

Next step was to wire up the speaker and fit it into the door. We had to use fat screws because of the slightly enlarged rivet holes. Note the cables coming out of the **09** grommet behind the speaker.

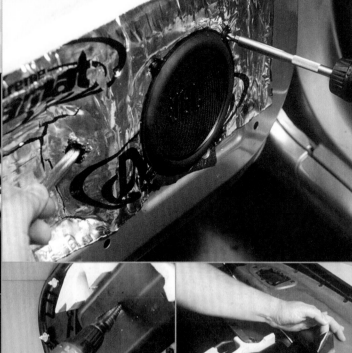

13 Once the mounting was tight, the tweeter was fitted. This eyeball mounting lets you angle the tweeter for best results, and we aimed ours slightly upwards towards the interior mirror.

14 The tweeter wire needed extending to the crossover, so we soldered another length of wire onto the short lead coming of the speaker.

15 We drilled this hole for the speaker wires to get them out to the JBL's crossover.

16 Once it was cut out, the wire from the tweeter was run along the panel and taped in place to stop it rattling about.

10 We decided to fit the tweeter higher up the door panel, so once we'd checked there was enough clearance for the tweeter mount, we drilled a pilot hole where the centre of the tweeter was going to be.

11 A holesaw was used to carefully chop a hole in the panel for the tweeter mounting.

12 The tweeter mount was pushed into the door, and the fixing ring was then tightened up on the reverse of the panel.

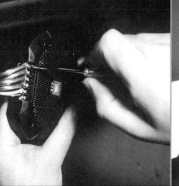

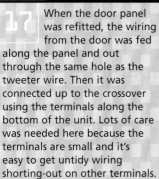

17 When the door panel was refitted, the wiring from the door was fed along the panel and out through the same hole as the tweeter wire. Then it was connected up to the crossover using the terminals along the bottom of the unit. Lots of care was needed here because the terminals are small and it's easy to get untidy wiring shorting-out on other terminals.

18 Finally the crossover was screwed in place on the door panel, tucked away in this small pocket.

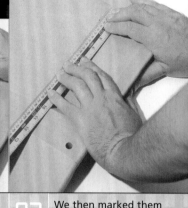

Rear
speakers

We decided that the standard Saxo rear speakers had to go. In their place we used an Auto Acoustics Stealth shelf made from MDF, with a pair of Sony 6x9s.

MDF shelves are heavy, so make sure yours is well secured. And be careful when fitting the plastic hinge blocks that locate it. They are screwed to the shelf and it's easy to strip the screws out of the MDF and stop the shelf fitting properly.

01 We started off by positioning the Sony 6x9 speakers where we wanted them to fit.

02 We then marked them up to give symmetrical mounting holes at each end of the shelf.

 Attention!
MDF dust is nasty stuff to breathe in. Wear a mask when you're cutting, drilling or sanding it.

07 Next we fitted the Sony speakers, using the pre-drilled holes to line them up. That was simple.

08 Finally, we fitted the speaker cable using push-on terminals, and tidied the wire up using P clips at regular intervals. The Neutrik speaker plug allows quick disconnection of the speakers should the shelf be removed.

09 Fitting the quick-release Neutrik plug and socket was easy enough, but we did one on the bench so that you could get a better look at it.

03 After drilling the speaker mounting holes, we turned the shelf over, marked the main aperture, and cut it out with a jigsaw. Doing this from underneath makes the cutting much easier than trying to do it from on top where the shelf is ridged. Once the holes were cut, we sprayed the underside of the shelf black.

04 Next we stapled pieces of acoustic cloth over the speaker hole to stop the carpet trim from sagging down once the shelf was covered.

05 After sizing the carpet to allow a decent overlap, the shelf was placed on its edge on the reversed carpet. We used spray glue to stick the two together, ensuring that we didn't spray over the speaker area, which could affect how they sound. Once the glue was sufficiently tacky, the shelf was laid onto the carpet, and the assembly turned over so that we could smooth out any wrinkles that might have appeared.

06 After flipping the shelf back over, we masked it up to give neat, straight edges to the trimming. We worked around the shelf, gluing and trimming the carpet edges until we had a tidy finish on each side.

Once you've threaded your speaker wire through the collar, and the correct size of clamp ring, insert each wire into its correct socket, and tighten the small screw onto the ferrule. After you've done them, you can push the bits together, and then screw the blue collar down onto the plug body.

Job one is to crimp the four supplied spade terminals to the wires that go to the amplifier, and put them onto the socket. The terminals in both bits of the Neutrik are marked to **10** help keep the wiring correctly lined up.

The plug requires a bit more work, but is still easy. Unscrew the blue collar from the plug and it falls apart. Then solder the four small ferrules **11** onto your speaker wires.

12 You can now begin to assemble the plug.

13

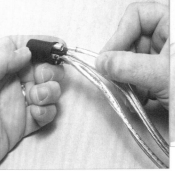
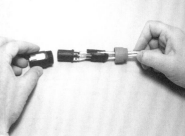

Sub woofer

To go with the decent front speakers that produce the mid range and top end, we need a bit of bass. Something to give the music some grunt, and that will test the bodywork on our Saxo. To do this we whacked a Dragster sub woofer into an Autoleads ready-made sub cabinet.

One thing we were careful about was screwing our sub cabinet in so that it didn't roll around. Not only can this be a real pain if the cabinet falls over and pulls the wire out of the terminal, it can be dangerous, particularly in a crash. The last thing you want when you're having an accident is a great lump of wood and speaker barrelling through the back seat and heading for you at speed. It might sound unlikely, but it has happened before and is very dangerous.

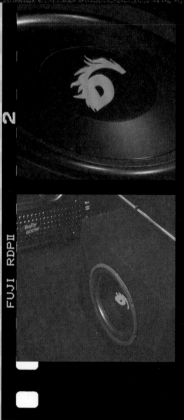

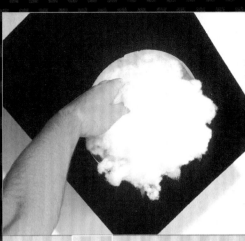

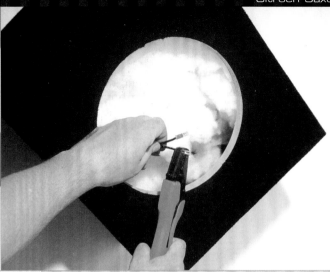

01 First the Autoleads pre-built box was first stuffed with wadding to help the speaker's performance. This is sold as toy stuffing, and is easily available from a fabric shop or haberdashery. It isn't expensive, and it does make a difference to the way the speaker works, so it's worth enduring the embarrassment of going into a dressmaking shop to buy it.

02 The wiring is already connected to the terminal cup inside the box, so the ends just needed stripping back and finishing off with the correct terminals to join onto the Dragster sub woofer. The cable is coded for easy connection.

After carefully positioning the sub woofer to get it straight, the eight mounting holes were drilled with pilot holes, and the screws were tightened steadily by hand to stop them getting stripped out. Don't slip when you're drilling or screwing.

03 If you damage the speaker cone it is not repairable.

Finally, the box was fixed into the boot with screws and L brackets. This is a vital job since the box and speaker weigh so much that they would be dangerous in an accident. You can also see that the wire from

04 the amplifier has been clamped under the cabinet's screw terminals. The cable was stripped back and heat shrunk, again for safety and tidiness. Make sure you leave enough copper wire uncovered to connect to the terminal.

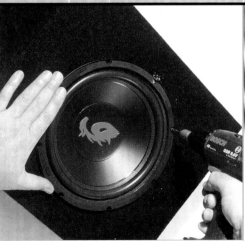

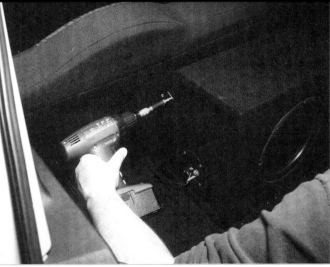

Wiring up

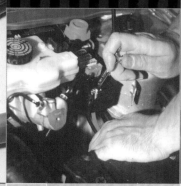

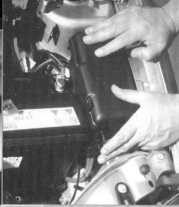

When wiring up a car audio system, it's very important to do everything properly and not bodge it.

The amplifier power wire must have a fuse fitted close to the battery, and you must use a grommet to protect the wire where it goes through the bulkhead. You must also keep the cable as far as possible from any of the car's wiring to stop any aggro with airbags, seatbelt tensioners and things like that.

The signal cable from head unit to amplifier also needs to be kept away from the car's wiring, as well as the amplifier power cable. Speaker wire is the least affected by its location, but it's a good idea to keep it away from the car's looms. Don't run cables over sharp edges that might cut into the wire...

01 The Saxo's positive wiring starts off at a weird quick-release battery clamp that doesn't allow adding any extra wires. Luckily there is a terminal that's just right for the job a few centimetres away in a main fusebox.

02 Having joined the new amp feed to this output, we then screwed the fuseholder into an easily-accessed position on a nearby relay box.

We cable-tied the new power wire neatly out of the way. The cable was easily fed into the car through an existing grommet, eliminating the need to drill new holes. **03**

This is where the fuse goes in, but we didn't actually fit it until we'd finished off the wiring and connected the amplifier up. **04**

The cables were run down the car as far away from the Citroën looms as possible. The signal cables went down the middle of the car, the power ran down the sill, and the speaker cables were also run down the middle. **05**

The power and speaker cables came together at the corner of the rear seat, where they were protected from the edge with lots of gaffer tape. The signal cables met up with the other wiring after it had been run across the boot floor, away from any interference sources. **06**

07 The terminals we used on the amplifier wiring were crimped on like this, starting with wire strippers to get rid of the wire's plastic outer insulation.

08 These special crimpers made squeezing the terminals onto the bare wire dead easy. Pliers like this are available at some decent motor accessory shops and car audio stores, so try and get the right tool for the job.

09 To keep things neat and safe we used heatshrink tubing over the joints. We could have used a heatgun to shrink the tubing, but we had a gas-powered soldering iron handy, so we used that instead. A quick blast of hot air from the iron's exhaust gives the desired effect, but be very careful not to touch the metal tip to the heatshrink itself, or it'll melt.

10 We had to cheat slightly with the Saxo's front speaker wiring because it ran through a multi-pin plug that stopped us running new speaker wire into the door. Instead, we joined the wire from the amplifier feed onto the front speaker wires at the head unit. We soldered this joint for the best connection, but if you've never soldered, you need to know how to do it.

11 When you need to join two wires, bare the ends back enough so that you can twist them together to give a strong join like these two here. If you're using heatshrink tube to protect the joint, don't forget to add it before you start soldering because you won't be able to get it on afterwards.

12 Once your iron is hot, melt a dab of solder onto the tip and place it against the joint area to heat it up. After a few seconds apply the solder wire to the iron tip and watch the solder flood through the joint. You need a smooth joint, not two pieces of wire with a blob of solder sitting on them. Keep the iron in place until the solder flows or you won't have a good connection.

13 To finish things off, a quick blast of hot air on the heatshrink makes a tidy joint that won't come apart in a hurry. If you haven't got heatshrink tube, insulation tape will do OK, just make sure that it completely covers all the bare wire.

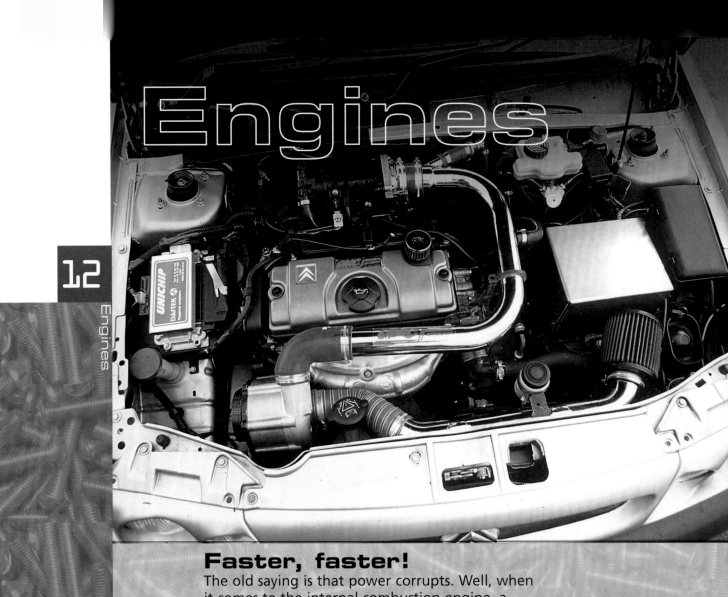

Faster, faster!

The old saying is that power corrupts. Well, when it comes to the internal combustion engine, a more apt saying would be that power costs. Lots. Serious power gains will cost serious cash. Unless you really spend a fortune and seriously modify your engine, you will not gain much extra power.

Fitting all the performance goodies in the world will be pretty pointless if the engine's is not performing as Citroën originally intended. Before setting out on the quest for more power, it's a good idea to perform a standard service - an oil and filter change, a new fuel filter, a new air filter (unless, of course, you're fitting an induction kit), new spark plugs and possibly HT leads (where fitted - only early models use them) and a check of the valve clearances (all models except the VTS) is the order of the day. Correct any obvious faults, such as hoses or wiring plugs hanging off, and look for any obviously-damaged or leaking components, too. For further information, refer to our Citroën Saxo Service and Repair Manual.

Minor mods (induction kits, sports back boxes and the like) might gain you a few horsepower here and there, and maybe even slightly-improved throttle response, but out-and-out power will be largely unchanged. Still the car will sound and maybe even feel faster. These "bolt-on" performance goodies have more effect as part of a "makeover" package. After all, you wouldn't want to be seen without a modified back box, and an induction kit certainly looks the part under the bonnet. Cosmetically very effective, but overall performance gains may be minimal - accept this and you won't be disappointed.

For those of you who feel the need for speed, it's really not worth starting with anything less than a VTR and preferably a VTS. That's not to say you can't tune the smaller-capacity engines, but it's definitely not the wisest way to invest your cash. After all, what's the point of throwing several grand at a 1.4 litre engine just to raise its performance to the same sort of level the 1.6 litre 8-valve VTR engine starts at? Having said that, if outright power is your main requirement, you're probably the proud owner of a VTR/VTS anyway. If that's the case, and you're prepared to splash the cash, then there are serious power gains to be had.

As with any mod, always be straight with your insurance company (see "Insurance" section). Mods like an induction kit are unlikely to affect your premium, but inform them anyway. Serious tuning work won't be taken quite as lightly, so expect the worst. As always, ignorance is no defence in the event of a claim.

An introduction to induction

An aftermarket air filter or induction kit will probably the first thing on your shopping list, after your big-bore back box. The idea of a filter or induction kit is to increase the flow of air into the engine, to help it "breathe" more easily. But surely the original induction system is designed to perfectly suit the engine? Of course it is - the standard system gives the best possible results achievable, whilst ensuring the incoming air is completely clean, and the stringent regs for noise and emission levels are met. Car makers have to make compromises - an aftermarket supplier's design brief is power, power and more power!

The theory behind an aftermarket air filter element or induction kit is that they allow more air to enter the intake manifold. Fuel and air must be mixed at a specific ratio (around 15 parts air to one of fuel) for optimum performance. Bearing this in mind, it follows that the more air you draw in, the more fuel you can supply with it. More air and fuel mixture equals a bigger charge entering the combustion chamber. A bigger charge equals a bigger bang, which results in a greater power output.

'If that's the case then, why don't I just remove the air filter altogether?' we hear you ask. True, that would result in maximum possible airflow, but with drastic consequences. The air filter is there to remove all the particles, large and small, and ensure a supply of "clean" air to the engine. Remove the filter element and your engine will end up swallowing dirt, dust, insects, rocks and maybe even small furry mammals. None of these will do anything to improve the combustion process, and will result in wear and damage to your engine. Not a great problem if you're running a touring car around Silverstone for 30 laps on a Sunday afternoon, but a bit more of a worry if you want to keep the engine happy and healthy for a few years to come.

As well as wanting more air, it is equally important that the air supply is cool. Cool air is denser than warm air, which is another important factor in increasing intake air capacity and therefore power. The original air filter intake is at the front of the car for this very reason.

Air filter element

It has to be said, not many MAXers go for just a replacement element, though they are available. The only reason for doing this mod would be if your insurance company won't let you have an induction kit. Or if you want to pretend your Saxo's totally stock. Hmmm. Another bummer with the Saxo air inlet system is that you really can't go drilling holes in the air filter box (like you can on other cars, to give it a throaty induction roar) - if you do, all that muck we spoke of earlier will have easy passage into your motor's innards. Not nice.

01 A replacement air filter is dead easy to fit - release the clips or remove the screws securing the air cleaner top cover . . .

On fuel injection engines, it may be necessary to disconnect the wiring plug from the airflow meter - this plug has a retaining clip, which can be released using a small screwdriver. Unclip the filter cover and lift out the old element. Before you fit the new element, carefully clean out the inside of the filter housing - use a damp cloth and make sure that none of the dust and muck goes into the engine.

Some performance filters have to be oiled before fitting - follow the instructions provided; don't ignore

this part, or the filter won't be effective. Fit the new element the right way up - it may have a "TOP" or arrow marking, or may only fit one way. If the filter won't fit, check whether you actually have the right one - don't force it in, and don't cut it to fit, as either of these will result in gaps, which would allow unfiltered air to get in. Refit the air cleaner cover, and secure with the clips and/or screws. On fuel injection engines, tighten the inlet air hose screw clip good and tight, or the system will suck in air where it shouldn't.

02 . . . and/or unscrew the screw clip securing the inlet air hose.

03

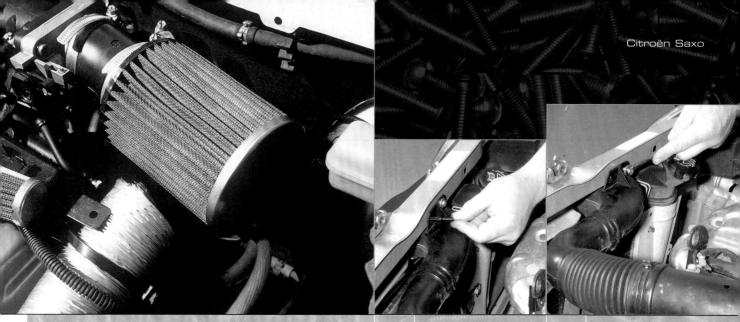

Induction
kit

So - an induction kit it is, then? Looks the part under the bonnet, and should show the best power gain (cold air ducting or a long tract kit is best for MAX performance), but is obviously more expensive. Once you've experienced the improved response and wicked roar, you know you won't settle for anything less.

01 First you need to remove the original air filter and ducting. Remove the plastic pin from the front of the ducting . . .

02 . . . then remove the three retaining bolts - two at the front of the car, and one on a bracket just before the ducting reaches the air filter housing.

03 Undo the screw clip from the main hose, and remove the two other hoses.

04 Lift the housing and the ducting from the engine bay.

>

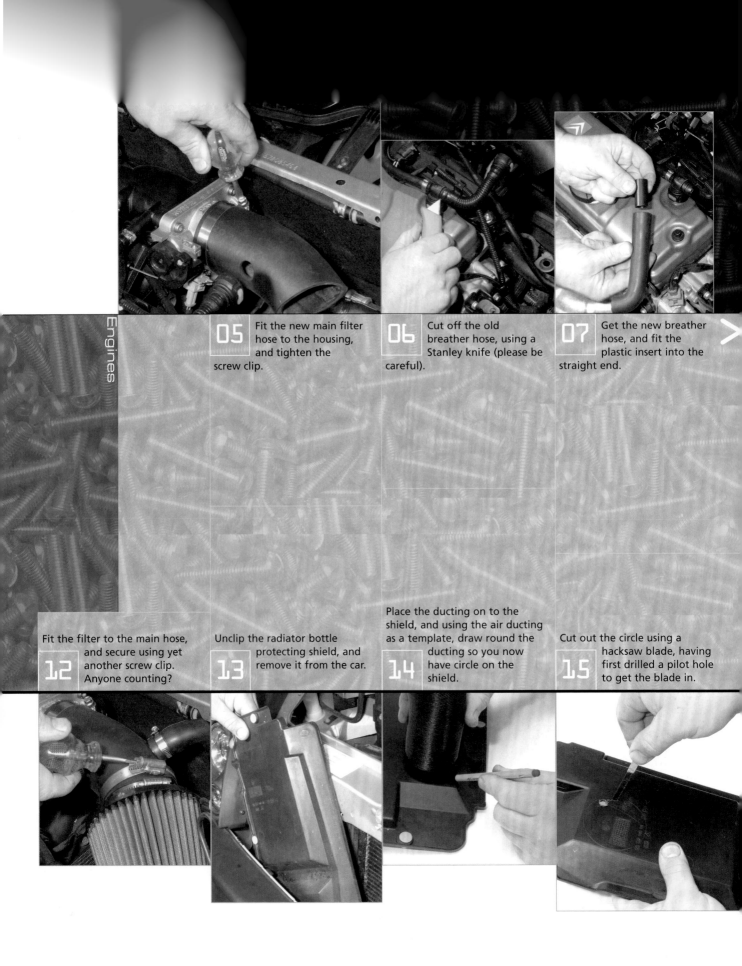

05 Fit the new main filter hose to the housing, and tighten the screw clip.

06 Cut off the old breather hose, using a Stanley knife (please be careful).

07 Get the new breather hose, and fit the plastic insert into the straight end.

12 Fit the filter to the main hose, and secure using yet another screw clip. Anyone counting?

13 Unclip the radiator bottle protecting shield, and remove it from the car.

14 Place the ducting on to the shield, and using the air ducting as a template, draw round the ducting so you now have circle on the shield.

15 Cut out the circle using a hacksaw blade, having first drilled a pilot hole to get the blade in.

08 Secure the insert by fitting a screw clip to the end.

09 Fit the new hose to the breather pipe, secure using a screw clip, and insert the other end into the main filter hose.

10 Fit another plastic insert to the rear hose (secure as before) and fit it to the main filter hose.

11 Fit the big plastic insert into the filter, and secure with a screw clip.

16 Insert the ducting from the back of the shield, and secure it at the front using a cable-tie.

17 Refit the shield, and thread the ducting back into the engine bay.

18 Secure the ducting to the metal heat shield, which is on the back of the radiator bottle, using a cable-tie to keep the ducting clear of the hot exhaust bits.

19 Feed the ducting round the side of the engine, and secure the end of the ducting to the bracket which originally held the old air ducting in place. You can also refit the front section of the original ducting back onto the car. This will assist feeding air to the new filter.

More show than go

All show and no go, yes, but you can't deny they look good. For those of you who like to spend time admiring what's under the bonnet, there's a wide range of accessories to tidy up and customise your engine compartment. Here's a rough guide to a few of the options available.

Customised rocker/cam cover

Another easy-fit item which is very effective at improving the appearance of your engine compartment. Covers only seem to be readily available for the 8-valve engines, but there's nothing to stop you spraying any cover you want - just remember to use heat-resistant paint if you want the finished result to last.

Battery and ECU covers

Simple to fit and very effective. Replace the naff plastic ECU cover with a more stylish alloy/carbon cover and fit a matching cover to the battery for an altogether more co-ordinated look. Especially when combined with a matching rocker/cam cover. You could even spray some items with heat resistant paint.

One thing to be wary of though - if you're installing a metal battery cover, ensure the battery terminals are sufficiently insulated and in no danger of 'shorting' out on the cover. A direct 'short' via a metal battery cover could result in your battery quite literally exploding and emitting a shower of battery acid over anything in its vicinity, ie. the engine compartment and quite possibly you. Nasty business.

HT leads

Not a great deal of point in changing your HT leads, because they're not the most visible thing under the bonnet - and that's assuming your Saxo's even GOT any. Don't be sold by claims that new leads will enhance your car's performance, either - unless the old leads are shot, you really won't see any improvement.

New leads are only an option on early models (except VTS) with a separate ignition coil and HT leads - VTS models and all other late models are fitted with "plug top" ignition coils of one sort or another. Lift the bonnet to see what you've got. If you can't see a separate ignition coil (on the left-hand end of the head) or any HT leads on the spark plugs (fitted to the rear of the cylinder head) you've got "plug top" ignition coils, and it's game over on the mods front.

Braided hoses

Turning your engine bay into something resembling that of a racing machine should only be done when the engine's completely cold to start with. Depending on which hoses you decide to treat, you could be removing ones containing hot coolant or fuel, and you don't play games with either, so be smart.

01 First step is to remove your chosen hose. If supplies of hose are limited, go for the hoses at the top of the engine first, then the ones underneath you can't see won't matter so much. Unscrew the screw clips, or use pliers across the tangs of the sprung-type ones.

02 Unroll your braiding, then expand it to the right size using a suitable blunt object. Like a screwdriver handle.

Slide on the hose clip and an end fitting. The hose clip is supposed to slide right up inside the end fitting, so it clamps the hose, the end of the braiding, and the end fitting (even when tight, the end fittings are still sometimes loose, though).
Slip the hose into place.
When you're sure the hose is fully onto its fitting, tighten the hose clip securely.

Fit the other hose clip and end fitting, then fit the other end of the hose and tighten the clip in place. It's pretty difficult to be sure the hose clip's in the right place on the stub - make sure it is, otherwise you'll have a very embarrassing leak. When you're done, remember to refill the cooling system (don't just use water - get some antifreeze in it) before you go out cruisin'.

03 Once the braiding's roughly the right size, you can slip your pipe in.

04 Trim off the excess, then smooth out the braiding round the bends, as it tends to gather up and look naff otherwise.

05

06

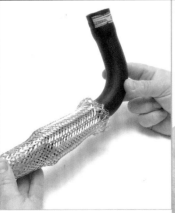

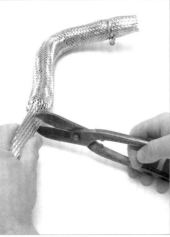

Attention!
If you are braiding coolant hoses, feel them first to make sure they're cold. Have a bowl ready to catch the coolant (Antifreeze is poisonous despite its sweet smell, and will make a mess of your paintwork if you douse the engine bay and front wings with it.

Exhausts

When it comes to exhausts don't be a fool and fit an exhaust trim - they'll fool nobody who really knows, and they certainly won't sound any better. Sort yourself out a decent back box upgrade, or as we did, fit a complete new system.

What a back box won't do on its own is give any noticeable power increases - although it'll certainly sound like it has. Check when you're buying that it can be fitted to a standard system - you'll probably need something called a reducing sleeve for a decent fit, which is a section designed to bridge the difference between your small-diameter pipe and the larger-diameter silencer. Try and measure your standard pipe as accurately as possible, or you'll have problems trying to get a decent seal between the old and new bits - don't assume that exhaust paste will sort everything out, because it won't.

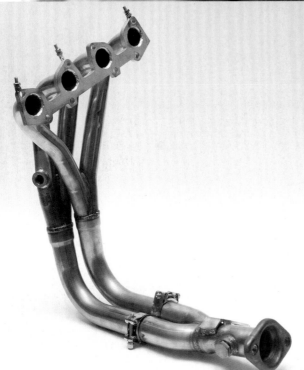

If you've got a capacity-challenged Saxo, you might need to lightly modify your rear bodywork to accommodate a bigger rear pipe (or pipes), and you almost certainly will if you get a bodykit done.

You will begin to see some useful power gains if you go for the complete performance exhaust system, rather than just the back box. Like the factory-fit system, the sports silencer will only work at its best if combined with the front pipe and, even better, the manifold it was designed for. There can be pitfalls here for the unwary, too - cheap exhaust manifolds which crack for a pastime are not unknown, and many aftermarket systems need careful fitting and fettling before you'll stop it resonating or banging away underneath. A sports rear box alone shouldn't attract an increased insurance premium, but a full system may do.

Don't go for too loud a system if you do a lot of miles, you might find the constant drone of a loud pipe gets to be a real pain on a long trip.

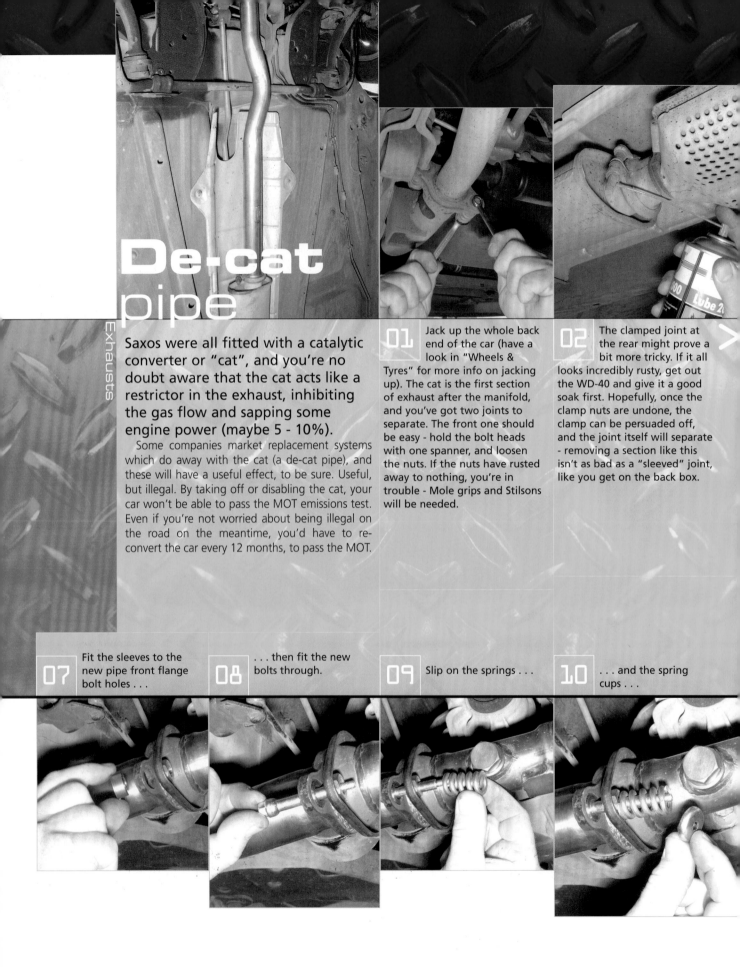

De-cat pipe

Saxos were all fitted with a catalytic converter or "cat", and you're no doubt aware that the cat acts like a restrictor in the exhaust, inhibiting the gas flow and sapping some engine power (maybe 5 - 10%).

Some companies market replacement systems which do away with the cat (a de-cat pipe), and these will have a useful effect, to be sure. Useful, but illegal. By taking off or disabling the cat, your car won't be able to pass the MOT emissions test. Even if you're not worried about being illegal on the road on the meantime, you'd have to re-convert the car every 12 months, to pass the MOT.

01 Jack up the whole back end of the car (have a look in "Wheels & Tyres" for more info on jacking up). The cat is the first section of exhaust after the manifold, and you've got two joints to separate. The front one should be easy - hold the bolt heads with one spanner, and loosen the nuts. If the nuts have rusted away to nothing, you're in trouble - Mole grips and Stilsons will be needed.

02 The clamped joint at the rear might prove a bit more tricky. If it all looks incredibly rusty, get out the WD-40 and give it a good soak first. Hopefully, once the clamp nuts are undone, the clamp can be persuaded off, and the joint itself will separate - removing a section like this isn't as bad as a "sleeved" joint, like you get on the back box.

07 Fit the sleeves to the new pipe front flange bolt holes . . .

08 . . . then fit the new bolts through.

09 Slip on the springs . . .

10 . . . and the spring cups . . .

03 Handle the old cat with care, especially if you've got any plans to refit it - dropping it or hitting it with large hammers shatter the ceramic inside and render it useless.

04 Clean up the joints front and rear with a wire brush.

05 With your new de-cat pipe, you should be supplied with new bolts, sleeves, springs and spring cups, etc, and a new sealing ring. Don't re-use the rusty old bits unless you're desperate.

06 Fit the sealing ring onto the front end of the de-cat pipe (the end with the two bolts), then offer up the pipe.

. . . before finishing with the nuts. Tighten the nuts gradually and evenly, each one a **11** bit at a time, until the springs are compressed.

12 Hook on the rubber mountings.

13 At the rear, slip on the top and bottom halves of the new clamp . . .

. . . then tighten the nuts **14** securely. Now consider yourself de-catted.

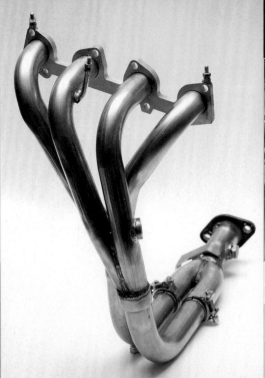

Four-branch
manifold

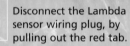

01 Disconnect the Lambda sensor wiring plug, by pulling out the red tab.

02 Unscrew the Lambda sensor from the exhaust downpipe.

07 Unscrew the downpipe mounting bolt from the bracket at the bottom of the gearbox.

08 Unscrew the manifold nuts and retrieve the nuts and washers. You'll need them to fit your new manifold - but, if they're obviously past their best, it's far better to source some new nuts.

09 Slide the manifold off the studs, then lower it down (careful - it's a tad on the heavy side) and remove it from the car, followed by its old gasket.

10 Clean up the area where the gasket was, removing all rust and muck that would prevent a decent seal. If you unscrewed any of the studs when removing the old manifold, don't panic. They can be screwed back in quite easily, using two nuts locked against each other - tighten them in so the studs are all roughly the same fitted depth.

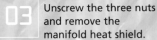

03 Unscrew the three nuts and remove the manifold heat shield.

04 Starting from the back of the vehicle, undo the back box clamp, unhook the mounting rubbers and remove the back box.

05 Remove the clamp, unhook the rubber mounting, and remove the back pipe from the catalytic converter section.

06 Remove the catalytic converter, as described in "De-cat pipe" previously.

11 Fit the new gasket, and try fitting the new manifold.

12 Ours wouldn't quite fit, so we had to grind out the mounting holes using a file - but don't overdo it.

13 Once you've finished grinding, fit the manifold and tighten the new nuts evenly and securely.

14 Install the mounting bolt at the bottom of the downpipe, under the gearbox, then finish off by refitting the manifold heat shield. Refit the Lambda sensor to the downpipe and reconnect the wiring, then refit the air filter and ducting. Then bolt the rest of the system in place.

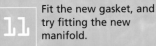

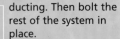

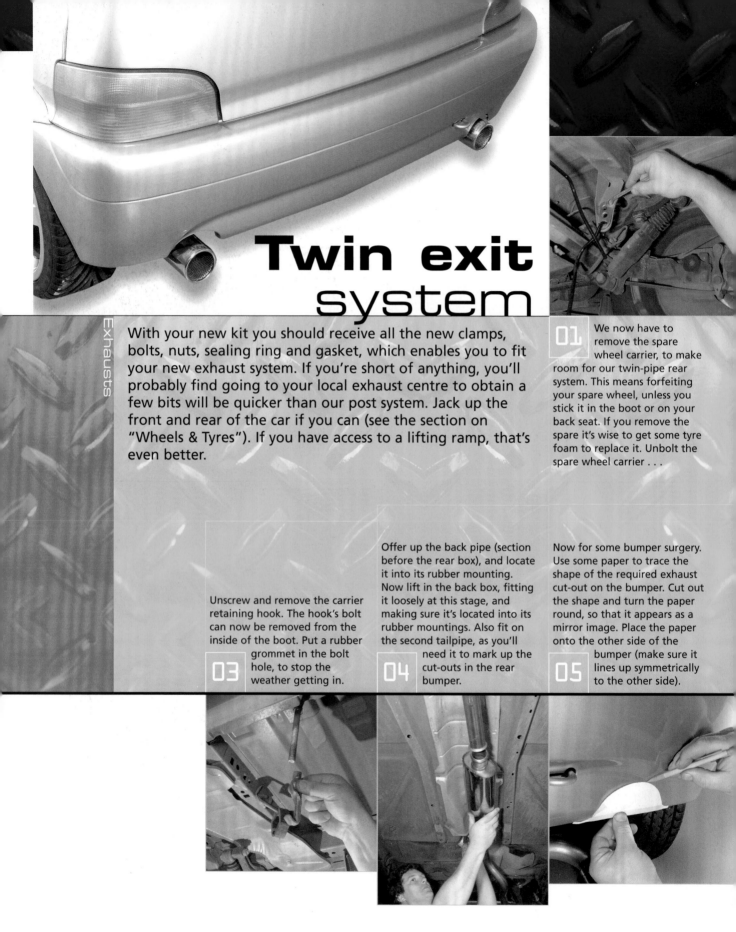

Twin exit
system

With your new kit you should receive all the new clamps, bolts, nuts, sealing ring and gasket, which enables you to fit your new exhaust system. If you're short of anything, you'll probably find going to your local exhaust centre to obtain a few bits will be quicker than our post system. Jack up the front and rear of the car if you can (see the section on "Wheels & Tyres"). If you have access to a lifting ramp, that's even better.

01 We now have to remove the spare wheel carrier, to make room for our twin-pipe rear system. This means forfeiting your spare wheel, unless you stick it in the boot or on your back seat. If you remove the spare it's wise to get some tyre foam to replace it. Unbolt the spare wheel carrier . . .

03 Unscrew and remove the carrier retaining hook. The hook's bolt can now be removed from the inside of the boot. Put a rubber grommet in the bolt hole, to stop the weather getting in.

04 Offer up the back pipe (section before the rear box), and locate it into its rubber mounting. Now lift in the back box, fitting it loosely at this stage, and making sure it's located into its rubber mountings. Also fit on the second tailpipe, as you'll need it to mark up the cut-outs in the rear bumper.

05 Now for some bumper surgery. Use some paper to trace the shape of the required exhaust cut-out on the bumper. Cut out the shape and turn the paper round, so that it appears as a mirror image. Place the paper onto the other side of the bumper (make sure it lines up symmetrically to the other side).

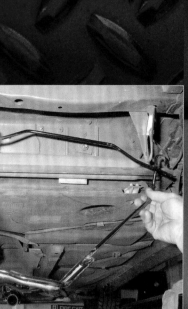

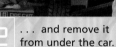
02 . . . and remove it from under the car.

Fitting a sports backbox

First we've got to lose some rusty bits. It's best to remove the nearside rear wheel for this, but it's not absolutely essential. Loosen the rear wheel bolts, then jack up the whole back end of the car, and take off the wheel. Have a look in "Wheels & Tyres" for more info on jacking up. First, loosen off the clamp nuts (hopefully, not too rusty - WD-40 works wonders).

Unhook the box from its two rubbers - these can be hard to get free, sometimes - use your largest screwdriver as a lever (some of that WD-40 might help, too).

Now all you've got to do is separate the pipes - ie split the box from the rest of the system. We won't try and pretend it's easy - large hammers, chisels and plenty of swearing are usually compulsory for this. Soak the joint in some more of that wonderful aerosol spray, and give it a few taps with a hammer. Usually, twisting the pipes relative to each other is the most successful way to separate them.

Before you go offering up your new silencer, clean up the joint area on the front pipe, then smear on some exhaust assembly paste. Put some inside the end of the new silencer too, if you like, but don't use too much, or lumps of it will break off and partly block your new free-flowing system - not good.

Slide on your new box, complete with a new clamp. Position the box by twisting it on the pipe, then tighten the clamp securely.

When refitting the rear rubber mounts, a little washing-up liquid helps them slide on (yes, really).

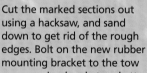
Cut the marked sections out using a hacksaw, and sand down to get rid of the rough edges. Bolt on the new rubber mounting bracket to the tow ring bracket and attach the rubber mounting to the tailpipe.

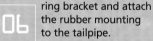
06

14 Safety and tools

Safety

We all know that working on your car can be dangerous - and we're not talking about the danger of losing your street cred by fitting naff alloys or furry dice! Okay, so you'd be hard-pushed to injure yourself fitting some cool floor mats or a tax disc holder, but tackle more-serious mods, and you could be treading dangerous ground. Let's be honest - we have to put this safety section in to cover ourselves, but now it's in, it would be nice if you read it…

Burning/scalding

The only way you'll really burn yourself is if your car's just been running - avoid this, and you won't get burned. Easy, eh? Otherwise, you risk burns from any hot parts of the engine (and especially the exhaust - if you've got one, the cat runs very hot), or from spilling hot coolant if you undo the radiator hoses or filler cap, as you might when you're braiding hoses.

Fire

Sadly, there's several ways your car could catch fire, when you think about it. You've got a big tank full of fuel (and other flammable liquids about, like brake fluid), together with electrics - some of which run to very high voltages. If you smoke too, this could be even worse for your health than you thought.

a Liquid fuel is flammable. Fuel vapour can explode - don't smoke, or create any kind of spark, if there's fuel vapour (fuel smell) about.

b Letting fuel spill onto a hot engine is dangerous, but brake fluid spills go up even more readily. Respect is due with brake fluid, which also attacks paintwork and plastics - wash off with water.

c Fires can also be started by careless modding involving the electrical system. It's possible to overload (and overheat) existing wiring by tapping off too many times for new live feeds. Not insulating bare wires or connections can lead to short-circuits, and the sparks or overheated wiring which results can start a fire. Always investigate any newly-wired-in kit which stops working, or which keeps blowing fuses - those wires could already be smouldering…

Crushing

Having your car land on top of you is no laughing matter, and it's a nasty accident waiting to happen if you risk using dodgy old jacks, bricks, and other means of lifting/supporting your car. Please don't.

Your standard vehicle jack is for emergency roadside use only - a proper trolley jack and a set of axle stands won't break the overdraft, and might save broken bones. Don't buy a cheap trolley jack, and don't expect a well-used secondhand one to be perfect, either - when the hydraulic seals start to fail, a trolley jack will drop very fast; this is why you should always have decent stands in place under the car as well.

Steering, suspension & brakes

Screwing up any one of these on your car, through badly-fitted mods, could land you and others in hospital or worse. Nuff said? It's always worth getting a mate, or a friendly garage, to check over what you've just fitted (or even what you've just had fitted, in some cases - not all "pro" fitters are perfect!). Pay attention to tightening vital nuts and bolts properly - buy or borrow a torque wrench.

To be absolutely sure, take your newly-modded machine to a friendly MOT tester (if there is such a thing) - this man's your ultimate authority on safety, after all. Even if he's normally a pain once a year, he could save your life. Think it over.

Even properly-fitted mods can radically alter the car's handling - and not always for the better. Take a few days getting used to how the car feels before showing off.

Wheels

Don't take liberties fitting wheels. Make sure the wheels have the right stud/bolt hole pattern for your car, and that the wheel nuts/bolts are doing their job. Bolts which are too long might catch on your brakes (especially rear drums) - too short, and, well, the wheels are just waiting to fall off. Not nice. Also pay attention to the bolt heads or wheel nuts - some are supposed to have large tapered washers fitted, to locate properly in the wheel. If the nuts/bolts "pull through" the wheel when tightened, the wheel's gonna fall off, isn't it?

Asbestos

Only likely to be a major worry when working on, or near, your brakes. That black dust that gets all over your alloys comes from your brake pads, and it may contain asbestos. Breathing in asbestos dust can lead to a disease called asbestosis (inflammation of the lungs - very nasty indeed), so try not to inhale brake dust when you're changing your pads or discs.

Airbags

Unless you run into something at high speed, the only time an airbag will enter your life is when you change your steering wheel for something more sexy, and have to disable the airbag in the process. Pay attention to all the precautionary advice given in our text, and you'll have no problems.

One more thing - don't tap into the airbag wiring to run any extra electrical kit. Any mods to the airbag circuit could set it off unexpectedly.

Exhaust gases

Even on cars with cats, exhaust fumes are still potentially lethal. Don't work in an unventilated garage with the engine running. When fitting new exhaust bits, be sure that there's no gas leakage from the joints. When modifying in the tailgate area, note that exhaust gas can get sucked into the car through badly-fitting tailgate seals/joints (or even through your rear arches, if they've been trimmed so much there's holes into the car).

Tools

In writing this book, we've assumed you already have a selection of basic tools - screwdrivers, socket set, spanners, hammer, sharp knife, power drill. Any unusual extra tools you might need are mentioned in the relevant text. Torx and Allen screws are often found on trim panels, so a set of keys of each type is a wise purchase.

From a safety angle, always buy the best tools you can afford - or if you must use cheap ones, remember that they can break under stress or unusual usage (and we've all got the busted screwdrivers to prove it!).

DO Wear goggles when using power tools.

DO Keep loose clothing/long hair away from moving engine parts.

DO Take off watches and jewellery when working on electrics.

DO Keep the work area tidy - stops accidents and losing parts.

DON'T Rush a job, or take stupid short-cuts.

DON'T Use the wrong tools for the job, or ones which don't fit.

DON'T Let kids or pets play around your car when you're working.

DON'T Work entirely alone under a car that's been jacked up.

Legal modding?
No such thing!!

The harsh & painful truth

The minute you start down the road to a modified motor, you stand a good chance of being in trouble with The Man. It seems like there's almost nothing worthwhile you can do to your car, without breaking some sort of law. So the answer's not to do it at all, then? Well, no, but let's keep it real.

There's this bunch of vehicle-related regulations called Construction & Use. It's a huge set of books, used by the car manufacturers and the Department of Transport among others, and it sets out in black and white all the legal issues that could land you in trouble. It's the ultimate authority for modifying, in theory. But few people (and even fewer policemen) know all of it inside-out, and it's forever being updated and revised, so it's not often enforced to the letter at the roadside - just in court. Despite the existence of C & U, in trying to put together any guide to the law and modifying, it quickly becomes clear that almost everything's a "grey area", with no-one prepared to go on record and say what is okay to modify and what's not. Well, brilliant. So if there's no fixed rules (in the real world), how are you meant to live by them? In the circumstances, all we can promise to do is help to make sense of nonsense…

Avoiding roadside interviews

Why do some people get pulled all the time, and others hardly ever? It's often all about attitude. We'd all like to be free to drive around "in yer face", windows down, system full up, loud exhaust bellowing, sparks striking, tyres squealing - but - nothing is a bigger "come-on" to the boys in blue than "irresponsible" driving like this. Rest assured,

if your motor's anywhere near fully sorted, the coppers will find something they can nick you for, when they pull you over - it's a dead cert. Trying not to wind them up too much before this happens (and certainly not once you're stopped) will make for an easier life. There's showing off, and then there's taking the pee. Save it for the next cruise.

The worst thing from your point of view is that, once you've been stopped, it's down to that particular copper's judgement as to whether your car's illegal. If he/she's having a bad day anyway, smart-mouthing-off isn't gonna help your case at all. If you can persuade him/her that you're at least taking on board what's being said, you might be let off with a warning. If it goes further, you'll be reported for an offence - while this doesn't mean you'll end up being prosecuted for it, it ain't good. Some defects (like worn tyres) will result in a so-called "seven-day wonder", which usually means you have to fix whatever's deemed wrong, maybe get the car inspected, and present yourself with the proof at a police station, inside seven days, or face prosecution.

If you can manage to drive reasonably sensibly when the law's about, and can ideally show that you've tried to keep your car legal when you get questioned, you stand a much better chance of enjoying your relationship with your modded beast. This guide is intended to help you steer clear of the more obvious things you could get pulled for. By reading it, you might even be able to have an informed, well-mannered discussion about things legal with the next officer of the law you meet at the side of the road. As in: "Oh really, officer? I was not aware of that. Thank you for pointing it out." Just don't argue with them, that's all…

Documents

The first thing you'll be asked to produce. If you're driving around without tax, MOT or insurance, we might as well stop now, as you won't be doing much more driving of anything after just one pull.

Okay, so you don't normally carry all your car-related documents with you - for safety, you've got them stashed carefully at home, haven't you? But carrying photocopies of your licence, MOT and insurance certificate is a good idea. While they're not legally-binding absolute proof, producing these in a roadside check might mean you don't have to produce the real things at a copshop later in the week. Shows a certain responsibility, and confidence in your own legality on the road, too. In some parts of the country, it's even said to be a good idea to carry copies of any receipts for your stereo gear - if there's any suspicion about it being stolen (surely not), some coppers have been known to confiscate it (or the car it's in) on the spot!

Number plates

One of the simplest mods, and one of the easiest to spot (and prove) if you're a copper. Nowadays, any changes made to the standard approved character font (such as italics or fancy type), spacing, or size of the plate constitutes an offence. Remember too that if you've moved the rear plate from its original spot (like from the tailgate recess, during smoothing) it still has to be properly lit at night. You're unlikely to even buy an illegal plate now, as the companies making them are also liable for prosecution if you get stopped. It's all just something else to blame on speed cameras - plates have to be easy for them to shoot, and modding yours suggests you're trying to escape a speeding conviction (well, who isn't?).

Getting pulled for an illegal plate is for suckers - you're making it too easy for them. While this offence only entails a small fine and confiscation of the plates, you're drawing unwelcome police attention to the rest of your car. Not smart. At all.

Sunstrips and tints

The sunstrip is now an essential item for any modded motor, but telling Mr Plod you had to fit one is no defence if you've gone a bit too far. The sunstrip should not be so low down the screen that it interferes with your ability to see out. Is this obvious? Apparently not. As a guide, if the strip's so low your wiper(s) touch it, it's too low. Don't try fitting short wiper blades to get round this - the police aren't as stupid as that, and you could get done for wipers that don't clear a sufficient area of the screen. Push it so far, and no further!

Window tinting is a trickier area. It seems you can have up to a 25% tint on a windscreen, and up to 30% on all other glass - but how do you measure this? Er. And what do you do if your glass is tinted to start with? Er, probably nothing. Of course you can buy window film in various "darknesses", from not-very-dark to "ambulance-black", but being able to buy it does not make it legal for road use (most companies cover themselves by saying "for show use only"). Go for just a light smoke on the side and rear glass, and you'd have to be unlucky to get done for it. If you must fit really dark tints, you're safest doing the rear side windows only.

Some forces now have a light meter to test light transmission through glass at the roadside - fail this, and it's a big on-the-spot fine.

Single wiper conversion

Not usually a problem, and certainly not worth a pull on its own, but combine a big sunstrip with a short wiper blade, and you're just asking for trouble. Insufficient view of the road ahead. There's also the question of whether it's legal to have the arm parking vertically, in the centre of the screen, as it obscures your vision. Probably not legal, then - even if it looks cool. Unfortunately, The Man doesn't do cool.

Lights

Lights of all kinds have to be one of the single biggest problem areas in modifying, and the police are depressingly well-informed. Most people make light mods a priority, whether it's Morette conversions for headlights or Lexus-style rear clusters. If they fit alright, and work, what's the problem?

First off, don't bother with any lights which aren't fully UK-legal - it's just too much hassle. Being "E-marked" only makes them legal in Europe, and most of our Euro-chums drive on the right. One of our project cars ended up with left-hand-drive rear clusters, and as a result, had no rear reflectors and a rear foglight on the wrong side (should be on the right). Getting stopped for not having rear reflectors would be a bit harsh, but why risk it, even to save a few quid?

Once you've had any headlight mods done (other than light brows) always have the beam alignment checked - it's part of the MOT, after all. The same applies to any front fogs or spots you've fitted (the various points of law involved here are too many to mention - light colour, height, spacing, operation with main/dipped headlights - ask at an MOT centre before fitting, and have them checked out after fitting).

If Plod's really having a bad day, he might even question the legality of your new blue headlight bulbs - are they too powerful? Keeping the bulb packaging in the glovebox might be a neat solution here (60/55W max).

Many modders favour spraying rear light clusters to make them look trick, as opposed to replacing them - but there's trouble in store here, too. One of the greyest of grey areas is - how much light tinting is too much? The much-talked-about but not-often-seen "common sense" comes into play here. Making your lights so dim that they're reduced to a feeble red/orange glow is pretty dim itself. If you're spraying, only use proper light-tinting spray, and not too many coats of that. Colour-coding lights with ordinary spray paint is best left to a pro sprayer or bodyshop (it can be done by mixing lots of lacquer with not much paint, for instance). Tinted lights are actually more of a problem in daylight than at night, so check yours while the sun's out.

Lastly, two words about neons. Oh, dear. It seems that neons of all kinds have now been deemed illegal for road use (and that's

interior ones as well as exteriors, which have pretty much always been a no-no). If you fit neons inside, make sure you rig in a switch so you can easily turn them off when the law arrives - or don't drive around with them on (save it for when you're parked up). Distracts other road users, apparently.

ICE

Jungle massive, or massive public nuisance? The two sides of the ICE argument in a nutshell. If you've been around the modding scene for any length of time, you'll already know stories of people who've been done for playing car stereos too loud. Seems some local authorities now have by-laws concerning "music audible from outside a vehicle", and hefty fines if you're caught. Even where this isn't the case, and assuming a dB meter isn't on hand to prove the offence of "excessive noise", the police can still prosecute for "disturbing the peace" - on the basis of one officer's judgement of the noise level. If a case is proved, you could lose your gear. Whoops. Seems we're back to "do it - but don't over-do it" again. If you really want to demo your system, pick somewhere a bit less public (like a quiet trading estate, after dark) or go for safety in numbers (at a cruise).

Big alloys/tyres

One of the first things to go on any lad's car, sexy alloys are right at the heart of car modifying. So what'll interest the law?

Well, the first thing every copper's going to wonder is - are the wheels nicked? He'd need a good reason to accuse you, but this is another instance where having copies of receipts might prove useful.

Otherwise, the wheels mustn't rub on, or stick out from, the arches - either of these will prove to be a problem if you get stopped. And you don't need to drive a modded motor to get done for having bald tyres…

Lowered suspension

Of course you have to lower your car, to have any hope of street cred. But did you know it's actually an offence to cause damage to the road surface, if your car's so low (or your mates so lardy) that it grounds out? Apparently so! Never mind what damage it might be doing to your exhaust, or the brake/fuel lines under the car - you can actually get done for risking damage to the road. Well, great. What's the answer? Once you've lowered the car, load it up with your biggest mates, and test it over roads you normally use - or else find a route into town that avoids all speed bumps. If you've got coilovers, you'll have an easier time tuning out the scraping noises.

Remember that your new big-bore exhaust or backbox must be hung up well enough that it doesn't hit the deck, even if you haven't absolutely slammed your car on the floor. At night, leaving a trail of sparks behind is a bit of a giveaway…

Exhausts

One of the easiest-to-fit performance upgrades, and another essential item if you want to be taken seriously on the street. Unless your chosen pipe/system is just too damn loud, you'd be very unlucky to get stopped for it, but if you will draw attention this way, you could be kicking yourself later.

For instance - have you in fact fitted a home-made straight-through pipe, to a car which used to have a "cat"? By drawing Plod's attention with that extra-loud system, he could then ask you to get the car's emissions tested - worse, you could get pulled for a "random" roadside emissions check. Fail this (and you surely will), and you could be right in the brown stuff. Even if you re-convert the car back to stock for the MOT, you'll be illegal on the road (and therefore without insurance) whenever your loud pipe's on. Still sound like fun, or would you be happier with just a back box?

It's also worth mentioning that your tailpipe mustn't stick out beyond the very back of the car, or in any other way which might be dangerous to pedestrians. Come on - you were a ped once!

Bodykits

The popular bodykits for the UK market have all passed the relevant tests, and are fully-approved for use on the specific vehicles they're intended for. As long as you haven't messed up fitting a standard kit, you should be fine, legally-speaking. The trouble starts when you do your own little mods and tweaks, such as bodging on that huge whale-tail spoiler or front air dam/splitter - it can be argued in some cases that these aren't appropriate on safety grounds, and you can get prosecuted. If any bodywork is fitted so it obscured your lights, or so badly attached that a strong breeze might blow it off, you can see their point. At least there's no such thing as Style Police. Not yet, anyway.

Seats and harnesses

Have to meet the UK safety standards, and must be securely bolted in. That's about it. It should be possible to fasten and release any seat belt or harness with one hand. Given that seat belts are pretty important safety features, it's understandable then that the police don't like to see flimsy alloy rear strut braces used as seat harness mounting points. Any other signs of bodging will also spell trouble. It's unlikely they'd bother with a full safety inspection at the roadside, but they could insist on a full MOT test/engineer's report inside 7 days. It's your life.

While we're on the subject of crash safety, the police also don't like to see sub boxes and amps just lying on the carpet, where the back seat used to be - if it's not anchored down, where are these items gonna end up, in a big shunt? Embedded in you, possibly?

Other mods

We'll never cover everything else here, and the law's always changing anyway, so we're fighting a losing battle in a book like this, but here goes with some other legalistic points we've noted on the way:

a It's illegal to remove side repeaters from front wings, even to create the ultimate smoothed/flushed motor. Sorry.

b All except the most prehistoric cars must have at least one rear foglight. If there's only one, it must be fitted on the right. We've never heard of anyone getting stopped for it, but you must also have a pair of rear reflectors. If your rear clusters ain't got 'em, can you get trendy ones? Er, no.

c Fuel filler caps have to be fitted so there's no danger of fuel spillage, or of excess fumes leaking from the top of the filler neck. This means using an appropriate petrol-resistant sealer (should be supplied in the kit). Oh, and not bodging the job in general seems a good idea. Unlikely to attract a pull, though.

d Front doors have to retain a manual means of opening from outside, even if they've been de-locked for remote locking. This means you can't take off the front door handles, usually. It seems that rear door handles can be removed if you like.

e Tailgates have to have some means of opening, even if it's only from inside, once the lock/handle's been removed. We think it's another safety thing - means of escape in a crash, and all that.

f You have to have at least one exterior mirror, and it must be capable of being adjusted somehow.

g If you fit new fog and spotlights, they actually have to work. No-one fits new lights just for show (or do they?), but if they stop working later when a fuse blows, relay packs up, or the wiring connectors rust up, you'd better fix 'em or remove 'em.

h Pedal extensions must have rubbers fitted on the brake and clutch pedals, and must be spaced sufficiently so there's no chance of hitting two pedals at once. This last bit sounds obvious, but lots of extension sets out there are so hard to fit that achieving this can be rather difficult. Don't get caught out.

i On cars with airbags, if you fit a sports wheel and disconnect the airbag in the process, the airbag warning light will be on permanently. Apart from being annoying, this is also illegal.

j Pace-car strobe lights (or any other flashing lights, apart from indicators) are illegal for road use. Of course.

k Anything else we didn't think of - is probably illegal too. Sorry.

Any questions? Try the MOT Helpline (0845 6005977). Yes, really.

Thanks to Andrew Dare of the Vehicle Inspectorate, Exeter, for his help in steering us through this minefield!

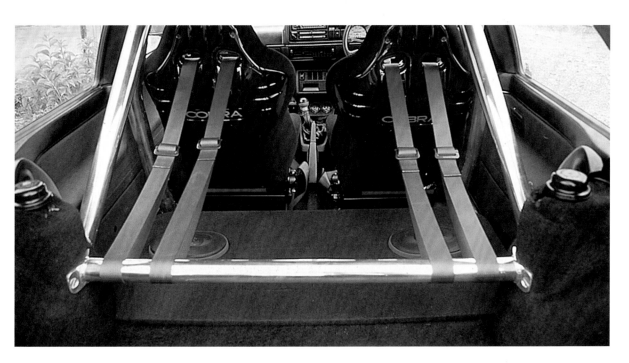

Thanks to:

We gratefully acknowledge all the help and advice offered from the following suppliers, without whom, etc, etc. Many of those credited below went way beyond the call of duty to help us produce this book - you know who you are. Cheers, guys! Roll the credits...

Britannia Cars
01443 490700

**Brown & Geeson
Distribution Ltd** (Momo)
01268 764411

Compomotive Wheels
01902 311499

Corbeau Seats Ltd
01424 854499

CT Racing
08000 283 284

Demon Tweeks
01978 663000

Eurostyling (Foliatec)
0208 987 5519

Halfords
08457 626 625

K & N Filters
01925 636950

Kits & Bits
01472 753711

LA & RW Piper (car trimming)
01935 851676

Larkspeed
08707 440101

Performance Parts Direct
01252 517272

Performance Products Ltd
01244 321300

R & A Design
01472 811711

RAID
01664 823792

Red Dot Racing Ltd
020 8888 2354

Richbrook
0208 543 7111

Ripspeed at Halfords
0845 609 1259

S.A.D. Motorsport (Ed)
(body styling)
01935 432352

Savage, Trillogy
01280 822865

Sedna Service Station
(body styling)
01935 850339

SPAX
01869 244771

Toyo Tyres
01933 411144

**A special
thankyou to:**
Brodie Baxter
Kim Baxter
Andy Butler (ICE words)
Zoë Harrison (ICE pics)
Jon Hill (cover shots)
Ellen and Alan Larkin
Bryn Musselwhite
Stewart Smith
Dan White (editor)

Haynes Car Manuals

Alfa Romeo Alfasud/Sprint (74 - 88)	0292
Alfa Romeo Alfetta (73 - 87)	0531
Audi 80 (72 - Feb 79)	0207
Audi 80, 90 (79 - Oct 86) & Coupe (81 - Nov 88)	0605
Audi 80, 90 (Oct 86 - 90) & Coupe (Nov 88 - 90)	1491
Audi 100 (Oct 82 - 90) & 200 (Feb 84 - Oct 89)	0907
Audi 100 & A6 Petrol & Diesel (May 91 - May 97)	3504
Audi A4 (95 - Feb 00)	3575
Austin A35 & A40 (56 - 67)	0118
Austin Allegro 1100, 1300, 1.0, 1.1 & 1.3 (73 - 82)	0164
Austin Healey 100/6 & 3000 (56 - 68)	0049
Austin/MG/Rover Maestro 1.3 & 1.6 (83 - 95)	0922
Austin/MG Metro (80 - May 90)	0718
Austin/Rover Montego 1.3 & 1.6 (84 - 94)	1066
Austin/MG/Rover Montego 2.0 (84 - 95)	1067
Austin/Rover 2.0 litre Diesel Engine (86 - 93)	1857
Bedford CF (69 - 87)	0163
Bedford/Vauxhall Rascal & Suzuki Supercarry (86 - Oct 94)	3015
BMW 1500, 1502, 1600, 1602, 2000 & 2002 (59 - 77)	0240
BMW 316, 320 & 320i (4-cyl) (75 - Feb 83)	0276
BMW 320, 320i, 323i & 325i (6-cyl) (Oct 77 - Sept 87)	0815
BMW 3-Series (Apr 91 - 96)	3210
BMW 3- & 5-Series (sohc)(81 - 91)	1948
BMW 520i & 525e (Oct 81 - June 88)	1560
BMW 525, 528 & 528i (73 - Sept 81)	0632
Citroën 2CV, Ami & Dyane (67 - 90)	0196
Citroën AX Petrol & Diesel (87 - 97)	3014
Citroën BX (83 - 94)	0908
Citroën C15 Van Petrol & Diesel (89 - Oct 98)	3509
Citroën CX (75 - 88)	0528
Citroën Saxo Petrol & Diesel (96 - 01)	3506
Citroën Visa (79 - 88)	0620
Citroën Xantia Petrol & Diesel (93 - 98)	3082
Citroën XM Petrol & Diesel (89 - 98)	3451
Citroën Xsara Petrol & Diesel (97 - Sept 00)	3751
Citroën ZX Diesel (91 - 98)	1922
Citroën ZX Petrol (91 - 98)	1881
Citroën 1.7 & 1.9 litre Diesel Engine (84 - 96)	1379
Fiat 126 (73 - 87)	0305
Fiat 500 (57 - 73)	0090
Fiat Bravo & Brava (95 - 00)	3572
Fiat Cinquecento (93 - 98)	3501
Fiat Panda (81 - 95)	0793
Fiat Punto Petrol & Diesel (94 - Oct 99)	3251
Fiat Regata (84 - 88)	1167
Fiat Tipo (88 - 91)	1625
Fiat Uno (83 - 95)	0923
Fiat X1/9 (74 - 89)	0273
Ford Anglia (59 - 68)	0001
Ford Capri II (& III) 1.6 & 2.0 (74 - 87)	0283
Ford Capri II (& III) 2.8 & 3.0 (74 - 87)	1309
Ford Cortina Mk III 1300 & 1600 (70 - 76)	0070
Ford Cortina Mk IV (& V) 1.6 & 2.0 (76 - 83)	0343
Ford Cortina Mk IV (& V) 2.3 V6 (77 - 83)	0426
Ford Escort Mk I 1100 & 1300 (68 - 74)	0171
Ford Escort Mk I Mexico, RS 1600 & RS 2000 (70 - 74)	0139
Ford Escort Mk II Mexico, RS 1800 & RS 2000 (75 - 80)	0735
Ford Escort (75 - Aug 80)	0280
Ford Escort (Sept 80 - Sept 90)	0686
Ford Escort & Orion (Sept 90 - 00)	1737
Ford Fiesta (76 - Aug 83)	0334
Ford Fiesta (Aug 83 - Feb 89)	1030
Ford Fiesta (Feb 89 - Oct 95)	1595
Ford Fiesta (Oct 95 - 01)	3397
Ford Focus (98 - 01)	3759
Ford Granada (Sept 77 - Feb 85)	0481
Ford Granada & Scorpio (Mar 85 - 94)	1245
Ford Ka (96 - 99)	3570
Ford Mondeo Petrol (93 - 99)	1923
Ford Mondeo Diesel (93 - 96)	3465
Ford Orion (83 - Sept 90)	1009
Ford Sierra 4 cyl. (82 - 93)	0903
Ford Sierra V6 (82 - 91)	0904
Ford Transit Petrol (Mk 2) (78 - Jan 86)	0719
Ford Transit Petrol (Mk 3) (Feb 86 - 89)	1468
Ford Transit Diesel (Feb 86 - 99)	3019
Ford 1.6 & 1.8 litre Diesel Engine (84 - 96)	1172
Ford 2.1, 2.3 & 2.5 litre Diesel Engine (77 - 90)	1606
Freight Rover Sherpa (74 - 87)	0463
Hillman Avenger (70 - 82)	0037
Hillman Imp (63 - 76)	0022
Honda Accord (76 - Feb 84)	0351
Honda Civic (Feb 84 - Oct 87)	1226
Honda Civic (Nov 91 - 96)	3199
Hyundai Pony (85 - 94)	3398
Jaguar E Type (61 - 72)	0140
Jaguar MkI & II, 240 & 340 (55 - 69)	0098
Jaguar XJ6, XJ & Sovereign; Daimler Sovereign (68 - Oct 86)	0242
Jaguar XJ6 & Sovereign (Oct 86 - Sept 94)	3261
Jaguar XJ12, XJS & Sovereign; Daimler Double Six (72 - 88)	0478
Jeep Cherokee Petrol (93 - 96)	1943
Lada 1200, 1300, 1500 & 1600 (74 - 91)	0413
Lada Samara (87 - 91)	1610
Land Rover 90, 110 & Defender Diesel (83 - 95)	3017
Land Rover Discovery Petrol & Diesel (89 - 98)	3016
Land Rover Series IIA & III Diesel (58 - 85)	0529
Land Rover Series II, IIA & III Petrol (58 - 85)	0314
Mazda 323 (Mar 81 - Oct 89)	1608
Mazda 323 (Oct 89 - 98)	3455
Mazda 626 (May 83 - Sept 87)	0929
Mazda B-1600, B-1800 & B-2000 Pick-up (72 - 88)	0267
Mazda RX-7 (79 - 85)	0460
Mercedes-Benz 190, 190E & 190D Petrol & Diesel (83 - 93)	3450
Mercedes-Benz 200, 240, 300 Diesel (Oct 76 - 85)	1114
Mercedes-Benz 250 & 280 (68 - 72)	0346
Mercedes-Benz 250 & 280 (123 Series) (Oct 76 - 84)	0677
Mercedes-Benz 124 Series (85 - Aug 93)	3253
Mercedes-Benz C-Class Petrol & Diesel (93 - Aug 00)	3511
MGA (55 - 62)	0475
MGB (62 - 80)	0111
MG Midget & AH Sprite (58 - 80)	0265
Mini (59 - 69)	0527
Mini (69 - Oct 96)	0646
Mitsubishi Shogun & L200 Pick-Ups (83 - 94)	1944
Morris Ital 1.3 (80 - 84)	0705
Morris Minor 1000 (56 - 71)	0024
Nissan Bluebird (May 84 - Mar 86)	1223
Nissan Bluebird (Mar 86 - 90)	1473
Nissan Cherry (Sept 82 - 86)	1031
Nissan Micra (83 - Jan 93)	0931
Nissan Micra (93 - 99)	3254
Nissan Primera (90 - Aug 99)	1851
Nissan Stanza (82 - 86)	0824
Nissan Sunny (May 82 - Oct 86)	0895
Nissan Sunny (Oct 86 - Mar 91)	1378
Nissan Sunny (Apr 91 - 95)	3219
Opel Ascona & Manta (B Series) (Sept 75 - 88)	0316
Opel Kadett (Nov 79 - Oct 84)	0634
Opel Rekord (Feb 78 - Oct 86)	0543
Peugeot 106 Petrol & Diesel (91 - 01)	1882
Peugeot 205 Petrol (83 - 97)	0932
Peugeot 206 Petrol and Diesel (98 - 01)	3757
Peugeot 305 (78 - 89)	0538
Peugeot 306 Petrol & Diesel (93 - 99)	3073
Peugeot 309 (86 - 93)	1266
Peugeot 405 Petrol (88 - 97)	1559
Peugeot 405 Diesel (88 - 97)	3198
Peugeot 406 Petrol & Diesel (96 - 97)	3394
Peugeot 505 (79 - 89)	0762
Peugeot 1.7/1.8 & 1.9 litre Diesel Engine (82 - 96)	0950
Peugeot 2.0, 2.1, 2.3 & 2.5 litre Diesel Engines (74 - 90)	1607
Porsche 911 (65 - 85)	0264
Porsche 924 & 924 Turbo (76 - 85)	0397
Proton (89 - 97)	3255
Range Rover V8 (70 - Oct 92)	0606
Reliant Robin & Kitten (73 - 83)	0436
Renault 4 (61 - 86)	0072
Renault 5 (Feb 85 - 96)	1219
Renault 9 & 11 (82 - 89)	0822
Renault 18 (79 - 86)	0598
Renault 19 Petrol (89 - 94)	1646
Renault 19 Diesel (89 - 95)	1946
Renault 21 (86 - 94)	1397
Renault 25 (84 - 92)	1228
Renault Clio Petrol (91 - May 98)	1853
Renault Clio Diesel (91 - June 96)	3031
Renault Clio Petrol & Diesel (May 98 - May 01)	3906
Renault Espace Petrol & Diesel (85 - 96)	3197
Renault Fuego (80 - 86)	0764
Renault Laguna Petrol & Diesel (94 - 00)	3252
Renault Mégane & Scénic Petrol & Diesel (96 - 98)	3395
Rover 213 & 216 (84 - 89)	1116
Rover 214 & 414 (89 - 96)	1689
Rover 216 & 416 (89 - 96)	1830
Rover 211, 214, 216, 218 & 220 Petrol & Diesel (Dec 95 - 98)	3399
Rover 414, 416 & 420 Petrol & Diesel (May 95 - 98)	3453
Rover 618, 620 & 623 (93 - 97)	3257
Rover 820, 825 & 827 (86 - 95)	1380
Rover 3500 (76 - 87)	0365
Rover Metro, 111 & 114 (May 90 - 98)	1711
Saab 90, 99 & 900 (79 - Oct 93)	0765
Saab 95 & 96 (66 - 76)	0198
Saab 99 (69 - 79)	0247
Saab 900 (Oct 93 - 98)	3512
Saab 9000 (4-cyl) (85 - 98)	1686
Seat Ibiza & Cordoba Petrol & Diesel (Oct 93 - Oct 99)	3571
Seat Ibiza & Malaga (85 - 92)	1609
Skoda Estelle (77 - 89)	0604
Skoda Favorit (89 - 96)	1801
Skoda Felicia Petrol & Diesel (95 - 99)	3505
Subaru 1600 & 1800 (Nov 79 - 90)	0995
Sunbeam Alpine, Rapier & H120 (67 - 76)	0051
Suzuki Supercarry (86 - Oct 94)	3015
Suzuki SJ Series, Samurai & Vitara (4-cyl) (82 - 97)	1942
Talbot Alpine, Solara, Minx & Rapier (75 - 86)	0337
Talbot Horizon (78 - 86)	0473
Talbot Samba (82 - 86)	0823
Toyota Carina E (May 92 - 97)	3256
Toyota Corolla (Sept 83 - Sept 87)	1024
Toyota Corolla (80 - 85)	0683
Toyota Corolla (Sept 87 - Aug 92)	1683
Toyota Corolla (Aug 92 - 97)	3259
Toyota Hi-Ace & Hi-Lux (69 - Oct 83)	0304
Triumph Acclaim (81 - 84)	0792
Triumph GT6 & Vitesse (62 - 74)	0112
Triumph Herald (59 - 71)	0010
Triumph Spitfire (62 - 81)	0113
Triumph Stag (70 - 78)	0441
Triumph TR2, 3, 3A, 4 & 4A (52 - 67)	0028
Triumph TR5 & 6 (67 - 75)	0031
Triumph TR7 (75 - 82)	0322
Vauxhall Astra (80 - Oct 84)	0635
Vauxhall Astra & Belmont (Oct 84 - Oct 91)	1136
Vauxhall Astra (Oct 91 - Feb 98)	1832
Vauxhall/Opel Astra & Zafira Diesel (Feb 98 - Sept 00)	3797
Vauxhall/Opel Astra & Zafira Petrol (Feb 98 - Sept 00)	3758
Vauxhall/Opel Calibra (90 - 98)	3502
Vauxhall Carlton (Oct 78 - Oct 86)	0480
Vauxhall Carlton & Senator (Nov 86 - 94)	1469
Vauxhall Cavalier 1300 (77 - July 81)	0461
Vauxhall Cavalier 1600, 1900 & 2000 (75 - July 81)	0315
Vauxhall Cavalier (81 - Oct 88)	0812
Vauxhall Cavalier (Oct 88 - 95)	1570
Vauxhall Chevette (75 - 84)	0285
Vauxhall Corsa (Mar 93 - 97)	1985
Vauxhall/Opel Frontera Petrol & Diesel (91 - Sept 98)	3454
Vauxhall Nova (83 - 93)	0909
Vauxhall/Opel Omega (94 - 99)	3510
Vauxhall Vectra Petrol & Diesel (95 - 98)	3396
Vauxhall/Opel 1.5, 1.6 & 1.7 litre Diesel Engine (82 - 96)	1222
Volkswagen 411 & 412 (68 - 75)	0091
Volkswagen Beetle 1200 (54 - 77)	0036
Volkswagen Beetle 1300 & 1500 (65 - 75)	0039
Volkswagen Beetle 1302 & 1302S (70 - 72)	0110
Volkswagen Beetle 1303, 1303S & GT (72 - 75)	0159
Volkswagen Beetle (Apr 99 - 01)	3798
Volkswagen Golf & Jetta Mk 1 1.1 & 1.3 (74 - 84)	0716
Volkswagen Golf, Jetta & Scirocco Mk 1 1.5, 1.6 & 1.8 (74 - 84)	0726
Volkswagen Golf & Jetta Mk 1 Diesel (78 - 84)	0451
Volkswagen Golf & Jetta Mk 2 (Mar 84 - Feb 92)	1081
Volkswagen Golf & Vento Petrol & Diesel (Feb 92 - 96)	3097
Volkswagen Golf & Bora Petrol & Diesel (April 98 - 00)	3727
Volkswagen LT vans & light trucks (76 - 87)	0637
Volkswagen Passat & Santana (Sept 81 - May 88)	0814
Volkswagen Passat Petrol & Diesel (May 88 - 96)	3498
Volkswagen Polo & Derby (76 - Jan 82)	0335
Volkswagen Polo (82 - Oct 90)	0813
Volkswagen Polo (Nov 90 - Aug 94)	3245
Volkswagen Polo Hatchback Petrol & Petrol (94 - 99)	3500
Volkswagen Scirocco (82 - 90)	1224
Volkswagen Transporter 1600 (68 - 79)	0082
Volkswagen Transporter 1700, 1800 & 2000 (72 - 79)	0226
Volkswagen Transporter (air-cooled) (79 - 82)	0638
Volkswagen Transporter (water-cooled) (82 - 90)	3452
Volkswagen Type 3 (63 - 73)	0084
Volvo 120 & 130 Series & P1800 (61 - 73)	0203
Volvo 142, 144 & 145 (66 - 74)	0129
Volvo 240 Series (74 - 93)	0270
Volvo 262, 264 & 260/265 (75 - 85)	0400
Volvo 340, 343, 345 & 360 (76 - 91)	0715
Volvo 440, 460 & 480 (87 - 97)	1691
Volvo 740 & 760 (82 - 91)	1258
Volvo 850 (92 - 96)	3260
Volvo 940 (90 - 96)	3249
Volvo S40 & V40 (96 - 99)	3569
Volvo S70, V70 & C70 (96 - 99)	3573

Haynes Car Service and Repair Manuals are available from car accessory retailers.
For further information or to find your nearest stockist, call
01963 442030 or visit
www.haynes.co.uk